Cambridge Studies in Social Anthropology

General Editor: Jack Goody

34

CHINESE RITUAL AND POLITICS

The God of Walls and Moats judging a wrongdoer

Chinese ritual and politics

EMILY MARTIN AHERN

Professor of Anthropology
The Johns Hopkins University

CAMBRIDGE UNIVERSITY PRESS

Cambridge
London   New York   New Rochelle
Melbourne   Sydney

Published by the Press Syndicate of the University of Cambridge
The Pitt Building, Trumpington Street, Cambridge CB2 1RP
32 East 57th Street, New York, NY 10022, USA
296 Beaconsfield Parade, Middle Park, Melbourne 3206, Australia

First published 1981

Printed in Great Britain at the University Press, Cambridge

British Library Cataloguing in Publication Data
Ahern, Emily Martin
Chinese ritual and politics. – (Cambridge studies
in social anthropology; 34).
1. China – Politics and government – 1976–
I. Title   II. Series
306'.2   JQ1516   80-41831
ISBN 0 521 23690 8

Religion and politics--China.
Rites and ceremonies--China.
China--Politics and government.

Contents

Figures

Acknowledgements

The bulk of this study was written in 1976–7 while I held a Fellowship for Independent Study and Research from the National Endowment for the Humanities. I am grateful for this support. I am also grateful to the faculty of the School of Oriental and African Studies, the University of London, who made their facilities available to me, especially Woody Watson and Sarah Allan, who extended warm hospitality and smoothed bureaucratic procedures.

A number of people have read and commented on portions of the manuscript at earlier stages, and I thank each of them: Maurice Bloch, Scott Guggenheim, Stevan Harrell, Beatriz Lavandera, Edmund Leach, Sidney Mintz, Richard Price, Sally Price, Stanley Tambiah, and Arthur Wolf. Special thanks go to Harold Scheffler for his detailed and encouraging criticisms and to Dennis Ahern for his painstaking commentary on the manuscript and insightful suggestions about its reorganization. Thanks also go to Paul Chen, Sue Naquin, and Howard Nelson for helping me track down various sources and materials. In addition I have had the benefit of comments during seminars at the Johns Hopkins University, the School of Oriental and African Studies, the London School of Economics and Political Science, Cambridge University, the University of Gothenberg, Columbia University and the Graduate Center, the City University of New York.

My fieldwork in Taiwan was supported during 1975 by a Fulbright Hayes Faculty Research Abroad Fellowship, a Social Science Research Council grant, and a National Institute of Mental Health Small Grant. I again thank the people of San-hsia for their patience in answering my questions, Liu Hsiu-yüan, my assistant, for her skill in analyzing Chinese society, and Wang Ch'un-hua for her help in gathering some important documentary materials.

Finally I thank Judy Salter for looking after my daughter in London, Barbara Curtin, Esther Graber, Kelly Heckrotte, and Karen Pekala for typing the manuscript, and Su-lien Hu for doing the calligraphy for the Character list.

Introduction

Some characteristic features of what we call ritual behavior are repetition, constant form over time, and exact specification of what participants should do or say. One or more of these features is usually present when animal ethologists, psychologists, anthropologists, or ordinary people use the term: for example, ethologists call attention to the stereotyping and fixity of form of 'ritualized' animal signals (Cullen 1972: 116); psychologists describe the 'ritualistic' repetitive behavior of neurotics (Mather 1970: 316); anthropologists analyze traditional and often unchanging 'rituals' accompanying birth, marriage and death; and any of us might speak of invariant 'ritual' routines, such as for getting out of bed in the morning or for saluting the flag. I shall use this broad definition in this book, focusing, in anthropological fashion, on those rituals that are patterned according to social custom and that involve more than one person in a social group at the same or different times.

My argument is based on Chinese material: in time I emphasize present-day Taiwan, and the latter part of the last imperial dynasty, the Ch'ing; in space I emphasize northern Taiwan and Fukien Province on the southeast coast of China, the original province (200 years ago) of the Chinese who settled most of northern Taiwan. The first-hand field data I include come from Ch'inan, a village in northern Taiwan, and nearby market towns, especially San-hsia.

As Wolf (1974a) and Feuchtwang (1974b) have shown, the three major categories of spirits in Taiwan, as in late Ch'ing China – gods (sin), ancestors (kong-ma), and ghosts (kui) – mirror the three social categories of government officials, kinsmen, and strangers.[1] All three sorts of spirits are regarded as persons: indeed they are all thought to have been living humans, who passed into one spiritual status or another after death. Being persons, each is believed to act on the basis of human-like reasons or motives suitable to his personal history and present status.

In the following Chapters, I pay closest attention to gods, the elites of the spiritual world. The kinds of eminence gods can display closely resemble the kinds of eminence living people can display. Gods can be famed as soldiers, as scholars, as doctors, or (especially goddesses) as paragons of virtue. Despite the

1

wide range of ways gods and goddesses can display their eminence, nearly all of them resemble bureaucratic officials. *Ma-co*, formerly a virtuous young girl, and *Co-su-kong*, formerly an official, both have temples whose architecture resembles a magistrate's yamen, subordinates who are called soldiers or runners, and processions that are organized after the fashion of magistrates' tours (see fig. 1 below). Even more to the point, most gods are thought to occupy the positions they do as a result of appointment or promotion within the spiritual bureaucracy on the basis of merit. This excerpt from the transcript of a spirit writing seance describes the process in the words of a god in central Taiwan:

My name is *Yen Lung*: I am a man of *Wan-an* who lived in the Ming dynasty. As a youth I went to the house of a master, and there studied both military and literary arts. At the age of 23 I came down out of the mountains as a knight errant, striking down the unjust, supporting virtue, and eradicating evil. I kept at these pursuits for 39 years. One day when I was 62 years old, I became involved in a fight with twenty-odd ruffians in order to save a young girl. Although I succeeded in saving her, I was grievously wounded, and not long afterward, medicine being of no effect, I died. In the underworld, the King of Hell graciously ushered me into the 'Gathering Place of the Good' (*Chü-Shan-So*), where I remained for five years. At the end of this period, I was enfeoffed as an Earth God. Later on I was promoted to be 'His highness Hsueh (*Hsueh Fu Ch'ien Sui*) . . .

Five years ago I was promoted to take over the position of Kuan Kung in this temple, which post I now occupy (Seaman 1974: 56).

As a spiritual official, a god is said to interact with other spirits, commanding lower-ranked gods and ghosts, and reporting to higher gods. A god can also interact with human civilians and officials, preventing injustice or aiding in administration of the empire (also at times mistakenly perpetuating injustice or bungling administration of the empire). The nature of gods as spiritual officials can be no more vividly summed up than by MacGowan's description of a young man who brought a petition before the image of a City God, beseeching the god to clear him of an unjust charge of theft and to expose the guilty person.

He took his stand in front of the idol, and the (images of) secretaries, with pens in their hands, seemed to put on a strained look of attention as the young fellow produced a roll of paper and began to read the statement he had drawn up. It was diffuse and wordy, as most of such documents are, but the main facts were quite plain.

Two young men were assistants in a shop in the city. Some little time before, the master of the shop, without telling either of them, concealed in a chosen place a sum of one hundred dollars, which he wished to have in readiness in order to pay for certain goods he had purchased. The previous day, when he went to get the money on the presentation of the bill, he found to his horror that it had disappeared. He had told no one of this secret hoard, not even his wife; and therefore he felt convinced that in some way or other one of his two assistants had discovered his hiding-place. For some reason his suspicions became aroused against the man who was now detailing his grievances, and who was appealing to the god to set in motion all the tremendous forces at his command, not only

1 and 2   A god and a magistrate carried in procession

3

to proclaim his innocence but also to bring condign punishment to the real culprit.

The scene was a weird and fascinating one, and became most exciting as the young man neared the end of his appeal. He called upon the god to hurl all the pains and penalities in his unseen armoury against the man who had really stolen the money.

'Let his life be one long torture,' he cried with uplifted hands. 'May every enterprise in which he engages end in disaster; may his father and mother die, and let him be left desolate; may a subtle and incurable disease lay its grip upon him; may misfortune pursue him in every shape and form; may he become a beggar with ulcered legs and sit on the roadside and beseech the passers-by, in sunshine and in storm, for a few cash that will just help to keep him alive; may he never have a son to perpetuate his name or to make offerings to his spirit in the Land of Shadows; may madness seize upon him so that his reason shall fly and he shall be a source of terror to his fellow-men; and finally, may a tragic and horrible death bring his life to a sudden end, even as I bring to an end the life of this white cock that I have brought with me.'

As he uttered these last words he grasped a chopper, and with one sharp and vicious blow cut off the head of the struggling animal, which wildly fluttered its wings in the agonies of death, whilst its life-blood poured out in a stream on the ground.

He then took his petition, and advancing close up to the secretaries, who seemed for the moment to gaze down upon him with a look of sympathy on their faces, he set fire to it and burned it to ashes. In this way it passed into the hands of the god, who would speedily set in motion unseen machinery to bring down upon the head of the guilty one the judgments which had just been invoked (1910: 139–40).

Soon thereafter it was said that the guilty man's beautiful sister was drowned, his family's farm was destroyed by flood, and he himself went mad.

The argument of this book is divided into three parts. In Part I I discuss what vocabulary we should use in describing Chinese ritual, concluding in Chapter 1 that it is crucial to distinguish those rituals that involve interpersonal communication from those that do not. In Chapters 2 and 3 I draw on two case-studies of Chinese rituals that involve interpersonal communications with non-human beings (often spirits), comparing the ways people attempt to control non-human beings through ritual action to the ways they attempt to control other people in ordinary life through political action. The comparison reveals many startling similarities: I argue that certain rituals can be analyzed as if they were forms of political activity, and that, as a consequence, the specialized vocabulary we have developed for describing interactions with spirits can, for certain purposes, be abandoned.

In Part II I take up some formal features of Chinese ritual, which include constitutive rules and restricted codes. These features will be examined in terms of Chinese divination, and then used to discuss the mechanism and form of change in Chinese ritual. In Chapter 4 I examine a number of forms of Chinese divination, arguing that divination involving interpersonal communication works by means of prearranged codes based on constitutive rules. This chapter thus

4

combines the distinction between interpersonal and non-interpersonal ritual introduced in Chapters 1–3 and the notion of constitutive rules. Two results emerge. First, having delineated the roughly bounded class of interpersonal divination, we will be able to specify some of its formal features. Second, we will see that some forms of Chinese divination are direct manipulations of systems of knowledge, whereas others are codes by means of which one can get access to the gods' superior understanding of systems of knowledge. Divination comes, then, in at least two radically different forms.

In Chapter 5 I suggest that the formal features of Chinese divination – and more generally Chinese ritual – bear importantly on the process of change in ritual. The mechanisms of change in 'closed practices', where conventions must be upheld unless they are deliberately changed outside the context of the practice, will appear very different from the mechanisms in 'open practices' where change can occur in an ongoing way during the practice itself.

Part III brings the lines of argument in Part I and Part II together. I start from the thesis of Part I, that acts intended to control Chinese spirits often parallel whatever acts are believed most effectively to control other people in everyday life. This is another way of saying that interactions with spirits will often be modeled on political processes. I then pose the question: whose ends are served by these parallels between ritual and politics? Two answers emerge. First (outlined in Chapter 6), some formal features of communication with spirits as described in Part II make them amenable to the ends of those *in* formal positions of authority in the Chinese state. Among other things, I evaluate recent claims that the arbitrariness and predictability of rituals make them useful to established authorities. Second (outlined in Chapter 7), other features of communication with spirits (as described in Parts I and II) make them amenable to the ends of those *outside* formal positions of authority. This contention rests on an examination of the kind of information about politics that is contained in Chinese ritual acts, information that includes exact details about how the political system works as well as useful strategies for dealing with it, and on an examination of the simplification inherent in restricted codes. I argue that the simplification common in Chinese rituals makes them analogous to learning games: when people carry out rituals modeled on political processes, they may be learning about politics itself. Finally, I speculate about the reasons why Chinese ritual has survived, in form if not in content, despite fundamental changes in the political order in both Taiwan and the People's Republic.

PART I

Interpersonal communication

1

Interpersonal versus non-interpersonal transaction

In this chapter I argue that in order correctly to convey the sense that a Chinese ritual has for the performer, one must often distinguish actions that involve interpersonal transaction from those that do not. One source for this distinction is R.R. Marett, who sets off mechanical causation from personal or quasi-personal agency (1909: 50). My conclusion — that a distinction of this kind is essential if a description is to convey the sense a Chinese ritual act has for the performer — is implicit in Marett's work, especially in his argument with Sir James Frazer over the distinction between magic and religion. Objecting to Frazer's claim that magic involves mechanical causation, Marett contended (as I will below) that much of what we label 'magic' is interpersonal: 'A magical transaction ought, hardly if at all less naturally than a religious transaction, to assume the garb of an affair between persons' (1909: 51—2).

Another source for this distinction is Hart and Honoré's study of British and American law (1959), in which they distinguish 'interpersonal transactions' from 'natural causes' in this way: interpersonal transactions, but not natural causes, 'involve the notion of one person intentionally providing another with a reason for doing something and so rendering it eligible in his eyes' (p. 54). For example, one might offer bribes or rewards, or make threats or demands, to give another person a reason for performing some action. The appropriateness of this distinction in the Chinese case is brought out forcibly by a distinction that Taiwanese themselves make between illness from 'within the body' and illness from 'being hit' (*chiong-tau*). Illness 'within the body' is caused by an imbalance in 'hot' and 'cold' or an excess of some substance (poison or 'breath'). Illness from 'being hit' is caused by a ghost, earth spirit, or other agent. The crucial distinguishing factor is whether an *agent* is involved: 'being hit' involves an agent and 'within the body' does not. It is for this reason that gods, who influence, order, exhort, and control other *agents*, are called in when illness is caused by 'being hit'. But when a god determines that an illness is caused 'within the body', he will usually refer it to a Chinese-style or western-style doctor, unless the god himself happens to be a skillful doctor. Sometimes people will bemoan the fact that an illness is 'within the body': 'if only it were "being hit" the gods would be able to do something.' Doing something about an agent who 'hits' is an example of interpersonal transaction; doing something about a substance 'within the body' is not.

In basing an analysis of ritual acts on this distinction, one would identify two distinct groups or categories: On the one hand, persons, person-like beings, spirits, animals, forces, objects, etc., who are thought to behave something like people do. They might be persuadable, controllable, enticeable, banishable; they might have intentions, goals, hopes, desires; they might be angry, sad, pleased, charmed, irritated; they might hurt, help, hinder, wreak vengeance, exact revenge. On the other hand, one would identify anything else in the social universe that people feel does not respond as a person would, and to which they would not attribute person-like behavior. Almost inevitably one would be describing a very wide range, in which there might be no sharp break at all along the way, but a gradual shading from fully fledged people on the one end, through quasi-human beings and spirits, to completely non-human entities on the other.

In the Chinese case one could describe in great detail the mode of interaction felt to be appropriate for gods, ancestors, ghosts, affines, landlords, neighbors, officials, and kinsmen of various sorts. One could also describe how rice-seed, rain-water, trees, animals, and a myriad of other things should be dealt with in a myriad of contexts. One would find a cluster of cases for whom the entire range of human approaches and responses would be felt to be appropriate as well as a cluster of cases for which this mode of interaction would not be felt appropriate at all. High officials, kinsmen, friends, neighbors, and most spirits are approached and respond in a largely human manner, though their characters differ. Some animals might be described as possessing only a few human-like characteristics and most other things – seed, tools, fertilizer, building materials, or plants – are not felt to be person-like at all. They are things only, and are not amenable to person-like treatment.[1]

In drawing up configurations of this kind, one would have to be sensitive to the presence of 'as-if' speech, in which objects felt to be entirely non-person-like are referred to as if they were persons. For example, we 'curse' machines and 'name' boats. Such things can happen in other societies as well and it is merely an empirical question in each case whether this is happening. One would presumably settle it by asking further: do machines *hear* our curses? Do boats have *preferences* for certain names? In this way one could eventually sort out what is said merely as a manner of speech and what is said because of the qualities genuinely imputed to spirits and things.

Let us consider how an analysis that began by sorting out roughly bounded classes of interpersonal transactions could be brought to bear on ritual acts in the Chinese case. As we will see in coming chapters, Chinese ritual acts directed to spirits take their logic from everyday interactions. They are not intended as 'naturally causal' and so they cannot be analyzed as such. For example, they should not be thought to produce the sort of causal effect produced when rice seedlings are irrigated. Instead, some are intended to have the sort of effects produced when a government office issues an order forbidding vehicular travel on a certain pathway. On the one hand, the order, issued by the appropriate body, in and of itself makes the regulation come into effect. This kind of effect is what Austin identified in performative utterances (1962: 5–6) and what Skorupski has recently discussed under the heading 'operative acts' (1976: 93).[2] On the other hand, the order gives people a reason for acting one way rather than another: they may or may not comply, depending on the inconvenience involved, the amount of surveillance likely, the sanctions applied and so on. As Chinese see it, the potency of ritual acts performed in this manner, as of government edicts, depends entirely on the power and authority relations involved. Chinese gods have power and authority over ghosts because of the positions they each have in a bureaucratic system. People can tap that power and authority if they directly implore the gods to act, obtain orders (charms) written and sealed on the gods' behalf, or hire a Taoist priest to act as the gods' emmisary. This potency might be called 'bureaucratic efficacy'.

Acts that are straightforward verbal or written orders can obviously be analyzed as interpersonal transactions, as can all attempts to persuade spirits by offering them things or showing them deference. But in Chinese ritual, less obvious cases can also be analyzed in an interactional mode. For example, sometimes ritual acts presuppose that the gods are able to respond intelligently to demonstrations of actions that people desire them to take. The man in the confrontation with the City God described above (pp. 2–4) killed a cock, explicitly and forcefully demonstrating to the god just what he hoped would happen to the guilty person. Justus Doolittle gives us an example of a similar kind from Fukien. When a child contracts smallpox,

on the third day after the pustules have begun to appear, it is a universal custom for one of the family to go to a baking establishment and procure ten small bits of Chinese yeast. These are steamed in the usual vessel for steaming rice belonging to the family. They soon begin to swell, and become several times larger than they were before steaming. These are then removed from the steamer and placed before the picture of the goddess, or whatever represents her majesty. The design of this operation is to cause her to exert her influence to have the pustules redden, fill up, and swell out, in resemblance of the swelling out of the balls of yeast when steamed (1966: I, 154–5).

On the fourteenth day, some black beans are roasted and presented to the goddess. Then the beans, which are thought to resemble the scars left by smallpox, are placed on the child's head and allowed to roll off (pp. 155–6). It seems clear that these acts are demonstrations to the goddess of what everyone hopes will happen: the pustules will first swell up just as the bits of yeast do; and they will then dry out and go away just as the beans do.

In time of drought, people use several sorts of demonstration to communicate to the gods their need for rain. In Doolittle's account of practices in Fukien,

11

the image of the Dragon King, 'Giver of Rain', is processed through city streets. In the procession,

one man carries a load of water in two buckets suspended from a pole laid across his shoulder. He holds in one hand a green branch of a shrub or bamboo with leaves, which he occasionally dips in the water, and then sprinkles the water dripping from the leaves around on the ground crying out, as he does so, 'The rain comes, the rain comes' (Doolittle 1966: II, 117).

Doolittle does not say explicitly that people intend these actions to show the god what they desire, though they might well. However, he does say that, in the case of extreme drought, they use another means to move the gods to action. An image of a god who is considered especially efficacious is

carried into the open court connected with the treasurer's office or with some other high mandarin establishment, and left there, exposed to the rays of the hot sun for a time. It is imagined that the divinity, thus exposed, becoming very dry and parched by this process, will feel the need of rain, and be led to expedite its falling from the heavens (1966: II, 119).

Sometimes props, like water or bits of yeast and beans, are manipulated to instruct the gods; at other times props are manipulated to deceive them. Arthur Smith tells us that 'the custom prevails in many parts of China, upon occasion of the spread of some fatal epidemic like cholera, at the beginning of the sixth or seventh moon to hold a New-Year's celebration. This is with a view to deceiving the god of the pestilence, who will be surprised to find that he is wrong in his calculations as to the time of year, and will depart, allowing the plague to cease. This practice is so well understood that the phrase "autumnal second month" is understood to be a periphrasis for "never"' (1894: 304). Because most gods would be thought too wise to be fooled by duplicity, such ruses are usually reserved for less powerful, evilly disposed spirits like ghosts. One can deter ghosts from doing harm to a child by taking measures to convince them the child is not worth taking: giving it away in pseudo-adoption, shaving its head in the style of a monk, calling it uncomplimentary names, or concealing its good looks with a mask (Doolittle 1966: II, 229, 316).

We can analyze another sort of act as a specialized kind of communication with the gods. Consider two practices reported by early travellers in China.

A person who swears falsely before the gods that he is innocent of charges brought against him consoles himself by means of an observance called Kai-yune. To check all the evil consequences which the gods may permit to overtake him, the perjurer writes on each corner of a clay tile the four following characters: Peng, Sew, Nga, Kai. He then places the tile on an altar in honour of the gods of the earth and rice fields. When several days have elapsed, he returns to the altar, and breaks the tile with a hammer. By this simple and ridiculous ceremony, he is supposed to avert all impending calamities (Gray 1878: II, 41–2).

It is very important that only 'good words' be said at New Year time. Children are specially warned not to use words of ill-omen, like 'demon', 'death', 'coffin', 'lion', 'tiger', 'elephant', or 'snake'. Lest they forget, or mischievously disobey, nervous parents stick up a red paper somewhere on the wall with the inscription: 'Children's words do not count'; or a placard over the front door reading: 'Heaven and Earth, Yang and Yin (the Male and Female principles), all things without danger from unlucky words.' Sometimes naughty little boys who refuse to curb their tongues and risk drawing poverty or ill-luck upon the household have their lips rubbed with paper money. Whatever they say is thus transformed into a promise of good fortune (Bredon and Mitrophanow 1927: 114–15).

I would suggest that these are conventional acts that serve to 'bracket' a communication with the gods, in Bateson's terms:

> Not only can the shoe of a horse stand for anything else according to the conventions of communication, it can also and simultaneously be a signal which will alter the conventions of communication. My fingers crossed behind my back may alter the whole tone and implication of everything . . . All messages and parts of messages are like phrases or segments of quotations which a mathematician puts in brackets. Outside the brackets there may always be a qualifier or multiplier which will alter the whole tenor of the phrase (1972: 230, 232).

In checkers a move is bracketed when a player leaves his or her finger on the piece after moving it. 'I make this move' becomes 'I make this move but reserve the right to retract it as long as I am touching the piece.' In the two Chinese examples above, communications to the gods are also bracketed: 'I swear that something is true' becomes 'I do not really mean to swear this'; all unpropitious words become their opposite.

As a final example, consider the Chinese notion that mentioning an event can bring it about. In some instances, the paradigm case is a person in authority who gives an order and expects to see it carried out: taxes are raised or a thief is arrested. Taiwanese make this explicit when they describe the 'good words' said by a woman's brother (or other males in her natal family, the *'gua-ke'*) at her funeral or her husband's. As he taps the nails on all four corners of the coffin he says good luck phrases such as, 'May the family have wealth and many sons'; people commonly say that whatever the *gua-ke* says will come about. It is clear they have a relationship of authority in mind as a paradigm: they say, 'The *gua-ke* has authority over us all'; 'just as anything the emperor says happens, so anything the *gua-ke* says happens'.

In other cases, the kind of authority the *gua-ke* has is not involved, yet describing a thing in words may make it come to pass. In one case I was told about, a child attended a ceremony at which an old man notified the gods he was about to start growing a beard. The child said, 'Grow a beard this year and die next year.' My informants said this actually came to pass. It is possible that words such as these are thought to produce an effect *by analogy* with cases where a person in a position of authority gives an order; the child is obviously not in a position of authority, but his words have the same effect they would if he were. In his analysis of magic, John Skorupski suggests this possibility, pondering whether the special magical connections he identifies as 'symbolic

13

identification' and 'contagious transfer' might be better understood as 'operative actions', 'signalling what is being done and thereby doing it' (1976: 153).

Another possibility is that utterances are thought to produce an effect by catching the attention of an evilly disposed ghost. Oddly enough one can see the pattern most clearly when words that are too propitious are thought to bring about their opposite. One can compliment a mother for having a 'beautiful' child, but not for having a 'plump' or 'healthy' one. The logic is that since it is a baby's health and plumpness rather than beauty that a mother cares about, a malicious ghost might seek to harm a baby if his attention is called to these qualities in it. In another example, after her recovery from a stroke, an old woman was furious with one of her kinsmen for commenting, 'Oh, I see you are no longer using a cane.' By calling attention to her good fortune he invited the attention of evilly disposed forces, who subsequently destroyed it. For all these Chinese cases, once we know a ritual act is transactional, the problems of what sense it has and what kind of effect it is meant to have are largely solved. On analogy with everyday transactions, orders are issued, reasons given, demonstrations made, communications bracketed, attention drawn, and so on.

In the Chinese case, it is clear that some acts involving spirits are not interpersonal transactions. For example, the elaborate methods adopted in Taiwan and China to ensure that certain events — weddings, funerals, laying the roof beam of a temple or ancestral hall — occur at propitious times, need not involve transactions with spirits at all. Before setting the date for such events as weddings, people consult hand-books of their own or seek out an expert, a geomancer, who, for a small fee, will consult his own books and advise them. Ordinarily, people and geomancers as well explain the 'unluckiness' of certain days by saying that various evilly disposed spirits are apt to be about. The local geomancer in San-hsia said, 'Bad days must be avoided for weddings and funerals because at those times gods, ghosts, and tigers are abroad and will clash (*huan*) with you, causing you harm. In one year there are 280 days unsuited for marriage, and forty unsuited for burial. If a day is bad because there is a white tiger around or some other rather insignificant entity, then pasting up a charm will suffice. But if other, more dangerous beings are abroad, nothing will do but to avoid that day.'

These dangerous beings are not present because of their own or others' intentions; they are there because of the operation of regular and predictable patterns in the nature of things. The geomancer explained with regard to detecting the presence of the *Thai-sin* (placenta god), a spirit associated with fetuses and infants who moves about the mother's room in a regular and orderly fashion: 'The movement is like the migration of fish: at certain times they are in certain places. It is also like the ripening of fruits and vegetables according to the season.' Neither men nor gods can fundamentally alter these orderly processes, though they can still control the activities of spirits to some extent: providing charms to prevent them from causing harm or — as in the case of one called *an-thai* (still-placenta) — to hold them in a certain place for a limited time.[3] Also they can and often do warn people against doing inappropriate things on certain inauspicious days. But the basic movement of spirits like *Thai-sin* and ghosts in time and space — whether *Thai-sin* will be in the wall at a certain time or whether many ghosts will be about on a certain day — is not the sort of thing that can be controlled by giving reasons or orders, or by persuading, enticing, or frightening.

Numerous other areas of Taiwanese life also fall outside interpersonal transaction. Chinese-style medicine is practiced on the basis of complex principles about the location and strength of *ch'i* (breath) and other entities in the body. These entities are affected by food, medicine, or manual manipulation (acupuncture) with no trace of interpersonal transaction. In Taiwan, just as one plants seed so it will grow into rice or vegetables, so one takes 'hot' medicine to offset a 'cold' illness. These are not the sort of things that enter into interpersonal relationships. Of course, these activities may involve some interpersonal transactions: one makes sure one has ownership of or rights to use a piece of land before planting it and one may ask the gods to influence the weather, which they control; one might take medicine to cure an illness as long as the cause was assumed to be 'within the body' and later ask the gods for a charm to exorcise a ghost, if that were determined to be the source of trouble.

I do not mean to imply that it is always possible to sort acts easily into or out of the class of interpersonal transaction. The class has rough edges. For example, people often make use of *'lou-nng'* — literally '(incense-) pot eggs' — portions of incense ash from the pot where incense sticks offered to the gods are placed. Sometimes these *lou-nng* are used to show spirits such as ghosts that one has the cooperation of gods. One first requests the god's permission to take a *lou-nng* to help control a problem ghost. If the god approves, the ash is then wrapped up inside a charm paper, also procured to help control the ghost, and displayed in an appropriate place. Just as the charm is a straightforward command to the ghost (more on this in the next Chapter), so the ash seems to be used to emphasize to the ghost the god's willingness to cooperate. In a similar way we might display a ring or other object that would prove we had the cooperation of its influential owner. As such its use is interpersonal. But at other times incense ash is requested in order to be used medicinally: it may be mixed with water and drunk or used in a bathing solution. The same substance can communicate a message to a sentient being or operate 'causally' to produce a mechanical effect on another substance. The same goes for charms: as we will see, they can be used as orders to spirits, or they can be burnt, the ashes mixed with water and drunk, as if they were medicinal.

2

Written bureaucratic communication

From this point on, I will use the distinction between ritual that involves interpersonal transaction and ritual that does not to restrict the phenomena I analyze. The following two chapters include two case studies of Chinese rituals that involve interpersonal transaction, which together will allow me to reach two conclusions. The first is that the specialized vocabulary we have grown accustomed to, reserved for interactions with spirits ('magic', 'charms', 'exorcisms'), can be shown to be often unnecessary and somewhat misleading when applied to Chinese activities. If a particular ritual is interpersonal, the appropriate vocabulary for its description is to be found in some sphere of ordinary life. The second conclusion is that interpersonal ritual, whether it involves interactions among human persons or between humans and non-human (i.e., spiritual) persons, often utilizes whatever ways of acting people see as most effective in controlling other people in everyday life. In the Chinese case, where there are formal positions of political authority, interpersonal ritual frequently involves forms of political control. This is a refinement on Durkheim's now platitudinous conclusion: that 'religious' objects, beings, and acts are modeled on society and its subdivisions (1915). The refinement suggested for the Chinese data is that at least some ritual acts involving non-human entities take their logic more narrowly from the political sphere. They put into operation ways of controlling other entities that occur in political acts in everyday life.

In the present chapter, I will conclude that Chinese written communications to or from spirits are hoped to have virtually the same kind and range of effects as written communications used among men: they can be used to store or transfer information and they can be used to bring the powers of incumbents in bureaucratic office to bear on a being someone wishes to control. For example, what have been called 'charms' can be understood as intended to have the same kind of effect as orders, mandates, or injunctions.

It is well known that written documents were extensively used for communication in China: without belaboring the obvious, I will detail some aspects of written communication among men in order to make possible close comparisons to written communication with spirits. I begin with written communications in

16

the official sphere, and then proceed to the sphere of ordinary citizens. In the Ch'ing, officials wrote petitions and memorials to other officials and the emperor and received the same in return.

A steady flow of returns, reports, memorials and proposed decisions in legal cases came into the provincial government from the *fu* or independent *chou*, as they did to each of these from subordinant offices. These were dealt with, according to competence in each matter, either locally or by transmission to the appropriate department in the capital, with other documents which they had themselves initiated. A flow of edicts, replies to memorials, new regulations, decisions on legal cases submitted, came back in the reverse direction for communication to the subordinant offices (van der Sprenkel 1962: 41).

In sum, it has been said that, 'Administration by higher provincial officials and by the capital offices consisted largely of the movement of paper' (Feuerwerker 1976: 63–4).[1]

Documents played a large role in interactions between officials and citizens outside the government as well. The district magistrate issued documents that could affect the local populace, from warrants for arrest to bills for taxes. Notification of taxes due went into two stages. First there was an official announcement of the dates on which tax payments were due. Then, one month before the due date, a document was issued to each taxpayer indicating how much he owed. Because of abuses that developed with this system, another sort of document began to be used in 1687, issued to the head of each *chia* division (official division of households) and circulated by him to each of the 5 to 10 households in the *chia* (Hsiao 1960: 95–6). When the tax was paid, written receipts, constituting legal proof of payment, were issued. In the case of default, written summons were used to demand a delinquent taxpayer's presence for flogging (Ch'ü 1962: 102).

Local elite could petition high officials for redress against local authorities, using the proper documents. At a time when the customary rate of exchange near the capital was 2,000 cash to one tael of silver,

A new incumbent magistrate increased the rate to 5,000, and this was quietly paid. Misunderstanding the temper of his constituency, after a few months, he raised the rate of exchange to 6,000. Then they grumbled, but they paid. A further increase to 7,000 provoked talk of organized opposition, but nothing practical resulted from it. Before the first half of his term of office had expired, he raised the rate again, demanding 8,000 in cash for an ounce of silver, or about four times the legitimate amount. This brought matters to a crisis. A mass meeting was held, at which it was decided to present a petition to the emperor, through the censorate . . . the documents were accordingly prepared and a committee of three influential literati carried them to the capital . . . It was returned to them unread, they were each favored with fifty blows of the bamboo, and fined a small sum for contempt of court. They returned home sore and crestfallen, and the local magistrate . . . signalized his victory by increasing the official rate of exchange to 9,000 pieces of cash for an ounce of silver . . . Another meeting was at once called, papers were more carefully drawn up . . . and another deputation bore them to the capital. This time they were successful. The offending official was degraded, stripped of his rank, and forbidden to apply for future official employment (Hsiao 1960: 123).

Ordinary citizens also entered the legal process by means of written documents. A petition to have a case tried had to be in writing and endorsed by the appropriate *ti-pao* (constable). Subsequently, the defendant would be required to submit a written defense (van der Sprenkel 1962: 66).

Documents properly drawn up and sealed were very powerful things: they might be used to subdue a criminal, bring about a conviction, hold someone to a bargain, or persuade a person in authority to take action on one's behalf. In the bureaucratic world, various means were used to increase their impact. Documents issued to inferior yamens as well as official notices, warrants, certificates, or papers relating to the delivery of funds or prisoners were embellished with a series of special characters written in red ink. The practice, called *piao-p'an*, involved adding characters such as *tsun* (obey) on official notices, *ching* (reverence) or *ch'eng* (sincerity) on sacrificial notices, *shen* (caution) on papers connected with the delivery of funds, *su* (haste) on a warrant, and so on. It also involved marking certain characters in the text of the document with red: characters such as *wei* (for the sake of), *cha* (document issued to an inferior), *kao-shih* (official notice), *shih* (order), or *yü* (instruction). A red circle was placed around *lin-tsun* (obey with awe) and *wu-wei* (do not disobey), and a red stroke marked along *yu-yang* (the order above is to be obeyed) (Ch'ü 1962: 249 n31). The items stressed seem related in an obvious way to the intent of the message: this is like our italicization. But the fact that the form of the markings was standardized served as testimony that the documents were authentic. *Piao-p'an* was done by the official or on his direct instruction.

Further measures were taken to insure trust in the authenticity of documents: it was important to issue them with the proper wax seal. In yamens this was the responsibility of a 'seal-attendant' who marked documents with the magistrate's official seal after insuring that they were properly endorsed by the magistrate and his private secretary (Ch'ü 1962: 78, 249 n30). The seal might also be used to prevent tampering with documents. On a warrant, the name of the runner assigned to deliver it was marked over with a seal to prevent a clerk from adding another name for his own nefarious purposes.

Of course, although documents were potentially effective under the proper circumstances, they also might fail: the accused might escape, or the authorities fail to act. In the example quoted from Hsiao above, a petition from local gentry to higher officials first failed and then succeeded in getting results. Also, despite the most careful preparation and sealing, documents were subject to ingenious methods of falsification. Hsiao presents a description given by a well-known nineteenth-century writer:

When the *liang-shu* [yamen clerk in charge of tax registers] made up the registers, he put on record, for each actual household [suitable for his purpose] an

18

imaginary one, which was supposed to be located in the same *t'u* and to have a head bearing the same name as the former, but which was liable for a different tax quota. This imaginary household was known as *kuei hu* [ghost-household]. Suppose a real household under the name Chao Ta was liable for one *shih* of rice; the *liang-shu* would make up a ghost-household, also under the name Chao Ta, but with liability for one *sheng* [1/100 of one *shih*]. When the time of collecting the taxes arrived, this *liang-shu* paid one *sheng* for the imaginary taxpayer, altered the figure 'one-sheng' to read 'one *shih*' on the receipt, and demanded from Chao Ta [the real taxpayer] the money equivalent of one *shih* of rice (1960: 107). [A '*t'u*' was a unit of 110 households.]

There were other reasons why a written document could fail to have its intended effect, even granted it was drawn up, embellished, sealed in proper form, and not falsified. A person, in officialdom or not, might attempt to persuade someone to take a certain course of action in an area where he had no authority to insist. For example, it was illegal for a magistrate to force the people to buy salt from licensed salt merchants rather than from smugglers; he could only issue a notice encouraging them to do so (Ch'ü 1962: 146). The ineffectiveness of these notices is made plain by the fact that magistrates usually could not sell their full quotas of salt (*ibid.*).

Lacking authority over the purchase of licensed salt, officials could only try to persuade citizens to obey their wishes. Similar efforts to persuade undoubtedly occurred often when a subordinate addressed his superior: when magistrates had to report serious legal cases involving sentences of penal servitude, banishment, or death to superior officials, private secretaries prepared reports on their behalf including a record of the inquiry, witnesses' disposition, and a statement of decision. 'The judgement had to be convincing and in accordance with law so that it would not be questioned and rejected by the superior official' (Ch'ü 1962: 10). The magistrate's success in having his decision upheld depended upon the persuasiveness of the arguments used.

In Taiwan today written documents function much as they did traditionally. An intense dispute between the Ong lineage settlement in Ch'inan and a wealthy businessman, across the river in Ch'ipei, illustrates this.[2] Tiu: was in the process of having a stone retaining wall built on his wide of the river to prevent erosion and flooding. This infuriated the Ongs, because they claimed the river had been moving ever southward, cutting into their land. They insisted that the very spot where Tiu: was building his wall was formerly Ong land, and that Tiu:'s wall would increase the southward erosion of the river, causing them to lose even more land. Further, they argued that a retaining wall had to be built on their side of the river first: since the width of the river-bed is set at a constant distance by government regulation, if Tiu:'s wall were built first, it would force the Ongs to build their wall on land that was not yet eroded.

In the playing out of this dispute, people produced and used numerous written documents. Early in the dispute, Tiu: sent his teen-age son to try to convince the Ongs not to make trouble. Ong Hai-a, the head of one Ong lineage segment, told him: 'We have official permission and a permit to build a wall here. The wall on our side must be built first.' Several days later the village head (*li-chang*), a member of the Ong lineage, called a meeting to which a representative of virtually every Ong household came. After hearing several passionate speeches reiterating the Ongs' position, everyone over twenty years of age signed and stamped a resolution stating the Ong case, addressed to the *hsien* (county) government. In two days a committee carried the resolution into Taipei and obtained permission from the *hsien* representative to present it to the *hsien* congress. The congress promptly decided to send a *hsien* official out to Ch'inan to look into the situation.

The same day in the afternoon the government officials arrived. Crowds of Ch'inan Ongs followed them about as they examined the wall-construction site. One man claimed he personally held the deed to the land Tiu: was building his wall on and defied him (in his absence, rhetorically) to produce proof of sale. Later the Ongs presented the officials with their trump card: their permit to build a wall on the south side of the river together with approval of a government grant for NT$24,00. Brandishing this, Ong Hai-a demanded, 'Why are they building first? If we aren't given redress, we will fight them.'

In the end, the Ongs did not fight Tiu:, but neither did they stop their efforts to influence the government. Two days after the site visit, Ong Hai-a wrote an angry letter to an official, accusing Tiu: of bribing government personnel. And about a week later, a new petition, testifying that the Ongs had lost land to the river and needed a new flood wall, was signed and sealed by all the Ongs. The effect of all these measures was felt a few weeks later when construction on two concrete and stone bulwarks began on the Ongs' side of the river. This was in the spring of 1970. By the time I returned in the spring of 1972, the Ongs had a massive embankment, stretching the entire length of the river adjacent to their land.

So far I have focused on documents used by or directed to officials. Now let us turn briefly to the use of documents outside official circles. In both Taiwan and traditional China, written contracts of a customary form were used to set out the terms of marrying, renting or selling land, loaning money, and selling goods. Notes drawn up when property was pledged as security in Ting Hsien, a district in northern China, ended with the statement 'Oral agreements cannot be depended upon, therefore this written contract is signed' (Gamble 1954: 256–7). Even gifts for ceremonial occasions were detailed in writing. People might prepare a gift list (*li-tan*) of the number and name of all items to be sent, place it in a special box, and send it along with the gifts. After the recipient decided which gifts he would accept, he returned an appropriate thank-you note (*hsieh-p'ien*) indicating whether he had accepted all, part, or none of the gifts and noting what sums were given as tips to the porters: sums that were fixed percentages of the value of the gifts sent (Kiong 1906: 60–1; 64–5).[3]

Among the many other examples of unofficial written documents, one must

20

suffice: visiting cards printed with one's name and perhaps other biographical information. They are, in Taiwan today, and were traditionally, extremely effective means of getting something done. It is well known that access to libraries, documents, government records or offices, and a myriad of other things is smoothed if one is in possession of a name-card from an influential person. Mere possession of the card, with or without anything additional written on it, is taken as evidence that the owner approves of one's activities. For this reason, Walshe urged prospective visitors to China to guard against their improper use. He recommended that some cards should be inscribed with a phrase on the back (*pai-p'ien* or *chuan-ch'eng pai-yeh pu-tso pieh-yung*) which indicated they were for ceremonial purposes only: these would be left as calling cards, for example. The plain cards, potentially open to misuse, 'should be kept as carefully as one's cheque-book, as they are very liable to be misappropriated by servants and applied to very dangerous purposes and should therefore be carefully locked up, together with the wooden stamp or "card plate" ' (n.d.: 42). In one case Walshe cites to bear out his warning, a missionary's card was used by a yamen policeman as proof that the missionary insisted he capture some brigands. When this proof was presented to the uncaptured companions of the brigands, they swore to exterminate the missionary whom they saw as responsible for the arrests and subsequent executions (p. 89).

I turn now to communications with spirits, beginning with non-official documents, to see what parallels can be found with the communications just enumerated. An essential part of every funeral ceremony in San-hsia is the reading of the *ce-bun* (sacrificial essay). It is a written document addressed to the deceased and read to him, usually by affinal kinsmen, though others may do so as well. The high status of affines at the funeral makes it appropriate for them to do this; I was told that an official, if there is one among the kinsmen, would serve equally well. The *ce-bun* 'tells the dead man what has been offered to him' by the person reading it. One *ce-bun* I saw began: '*Ci-hu* [elder sister's husband] , I am sorry I came too late to see you. We have prepared [so many] bundles of paper money and [so many] offerings of three cooked kinds for you.' De Groot gives a description of a *ce-bun* used in Amoy, Fukien: like the Taiwan version, it informed the deceased what offerings were brought for him (1885: 52–64). He also mentions that as mourners departed, each was given a document thanking him for the portion of his offering to the deceased that was accepted, and stating respectfully what portion was returned (p. 70).

The *ce-bun* functions much like a gift list. In ordinary life one makes a record of how many gifts are delivered, both to cover loss in transit (How much more risky is transit to the world of the dead!) and to prove that one's obligations to the recipient are satisfied. The *ce-bun* plays some part in satisfying the deceased. People said that without it he would not know how much was offered to him, implying that this would make him unhappy. The authority of the affines (or an official) is mustered to put force into the announcement, and the reading is

21

immediately followed by a exorcistic ritual expressing the desire of the living that the deceased will not return to bother them.[4] In Amoy, the *ce-bun* was complemented by the funeral thank-you note, just as the gift list must often have been complemented by its thank-you note, the *hsieh-p'ien*.

Still other documents may accompany the funeral ceremony, which parallel the communications among officials or between citizens and officials discussed above. In San-hsia, Taoist priests help prepare certain documents for the 'merit ceremony' (*kong-tiek*), which is often held in the evening of the day the *ce-bun* is read. A knowledgeable elderly man in the village explained:

First the Taoist priest calls upon the gods to come and tell what crimes or wrongs the dead man has committed. Then the head of the clan organization reads a pronouncement addressed to a god who then goes to heaven and asks pardon for the dead man's wrongs. If you have done some bad thing, it becomes as if you had never done it. The pronouncement states the place of origin of [our kinsmen] on the mainland, where the dead man lives now, the names and death dates of all the dead for whom the merit ceremony is being done, and instructions to eradicate the wrongs of the dead. It is essential that this be read by a man who is or has been an official. Since the clan head used to be the mayor of San-hsia town, he could read it.

This document is meant to function much like any report from a subordinate official requesting some action. In this case the action requested is a pardoning of misdeeds, something that was within the authority both of the emperor and of the highest gods in heaven. The document must be read by a person with official status because the gods are being asked to act in an official capacity: in this bureaucratic system, documents must not only be prepared correctly, they must be presented by the proper people. If no official or former official is available, the Taoist priest himself will present the document, in his capacity as 'mandarin of the gods' (see below). In contrast, the *ce-bun* is read by someone whose authority will impress the deceased, but it may well have the desired effect no matter who reads it. After all, it is only intended to convey information to the deceased.

Other funeral documents reveal further similarities to the way official documents function: at the end of the *kong-tiek* ceremonies a document much like the *ce-bun* is read, listing all the ceremonies performed on behalf of the deceased and all the descendants whom the deceased left behind. It is embellished with red circles, just as in the practice of *piao-p'an*.

People say the effect of the merit ceremonies as a whole is to erase any wrongs the deceased may have done. But this effect is a result of that part of the proceedings people describe as 'most essential': when a written request for a pardon is presented to the high heavenly authorities by a subordinate. Its effect, if secured, is a function of those high authorities exercising a prerogative (to pardon crime) attached to their offices. The centrality of this part of the proceedings is brought out by an anecdote one man told me: when his father gave a *kong-tiek* ceremony for one of his ancestors he included the names of all the other ancestors who had not previously had a merit ceremony performed for them, except for one which he omitted. Just before the ceremony began, he felt stones hitting against his body. Remembering the name he had omitted, he said, 'Is that you, grandmother?' At this the stones came even faster. After he wrote her name down the stones stopped hitting him. My informant pointed out that if his grandmother's name had not been written down on the proper document before the ceremony, she would not have received its benefits.

More esoteric rituals like the *chiao*, performed largely by Taoists within a temple, also include written documents intended for spiritual officials. Ethnographic descriptions of this rite by anthropologists learned in Taoist intricacies make this clear. First of all, the Taoist priest occupies a position intermediate between ordinary citizens and the higher sources of power in the bureaucratic spiritual hierarchy. So, as Michael Saso points out, the Taoist robe has 'the official belt of a mandarin . . . embroidered around the center, showing that the Taoist is a heavenly official, mediator between the rule of the gods and man' (1972: 40). His cap and attached crown are called '*Chin Kuan*' or gold crown. 'The word *Kuan* or crown is used to describe the headpiece of an official demonstrating that the Taoist is a mandarin in the offices of the heavenly rulers. To the common folk, therefore, a Taoist is by definition a mandarin official of the spirits' (1972: 40–1).

In the latter part of the first ceremony of the *chiao*, the gods are summoned to attend. 'One by one, 280 or 360 spirits are invited to be present for the *Chiao*, and a great document called a *Tieh*, an official dispatch, is sent to Heaven to accomplish the invitation' (Saso 1972: 66). As a part of the next phase, during which the central ritual area is purified, there is a 'sending off of the talisman' which is regarded as 'a contractual treaty with the spirits of the Prior Heavens. The treaty will be signed and ratified during the coming ritual acts of the *Chiao* festival' (Saso 1972: 70).

On the third day comes the 'Presentation of the memorial', a document that contains 'the names of all the villagers, their petitions and a summation of the rites of the *Chiao* festival' (Saso 1972: 44). In Schipper's analysis of such a memorial, he argues convincingly that it is intended to put the workings of a bureaucracy into effect. At one point the document reads, 'with sincere fear and apprehension, bowing and knocking his head in a hundred-fold salute, the aforenamed servant humbly presents this memorial on behalf of the population of *A-lien*' (1974: 314–15). Schipper comments, 'The expression of apprehension and humility is a standard formula found not only in this kind of Taoist literature, but also in similar documents of the imperial administration' (p. 317).

Continuing the bureaucratic idiom, one of the last acts of the *chiao* is the posting of a huge red document (*pang*) on the temple wall, containing a list of names of everyone who was involved in or contributed to the cost of the *chiao*. 'Their names are posted as if they were literati who had passed the imperial examinations and attained the ranks of immortals in the Prior Heavens' (Saso

1972: 83). And last, 'each family takes home a yellow document, bearing the seal of the Taoist, which describes the contract with the heavens [to protect them]' (p. 44). The parallels between these ritual documents and those used in dealing with the earthly bureaucracy, in both the form they take and the effect they are intended to have, should be obvious.

Charms, *hu*, are also used to communicate between men and spiritual officials, for the special purpose of controlling a third party, be it man or spirit. One obtains a charm from a spiritual official or his delegate and brings the command it contains to bear on the third party one wishes to control. 'Paper charms embody commands from higher ranking gods to lower ranking spirits or human beings. Properly drawn, activated, and sealed, they exercise the gods' authority in a way precisely analogous to the way in which secular legal documents exercise political authority among men' (McCreery 1973: 107).

De Groot gives us some examples from Amoy:

'It is ordered that General *Li Kwang* shall shoot his arrows here.' This man was a hero of the second century before our era, who rendered himself famous by victorious campaigns against the Huns. 'This is an order to the Primordial Women of the Nine Heavens to supress murderous influences.' 'Deified prince ruling the years (the planet Jupiter), take station here' (1969: VI, 1045).

Cormack describes a similar charm for the cure of a cough: 'The god of Thunder is hereby specially ordered to take his mallet and chisel and strike with the thunder-bolt the king of demons, all mischievous specters, and the malignant stellar gods who cause infirmities and ailments' (1922: 218). Some final examples come from Taiwan. A 'cleansing charm' would be read: 'Heaven and Earth, the Lord of Thunder, and all the gods of the three religions of China with all their terrific power command the god of the year and the gods of the months and hours to dispel whatever evil powers threaten here' (McCreery 1973: 111). A more modest charm I saw attached to the mosquito net on the bed of a woman whose labor was overdue said simply, 'Son inside the mother's body, come out!'[5]

The words spoken when a charm is prepared reinforce its bureaucratic impact. Ritual specialists of the Lü-shan sect in Taiwan say the following while preparing a charm used in rituals to recall a person's soul:

Our teacher issues an imperial edict on my behalf; the ancestors issue an imperial edict on my behalf; the immortals issue an imperial edict on my behalf . . . Ward off! Go! Evil spirits and malicious forces flee without stopping. I receive the orders of the great Lord Lao: the god's soldiers will act quickly as if they had received a legal order (Liu 1974: 226).[6]

Charms are efforts to confront evilly disposed beings with the superior authority of gods, through the ordinary bureaucratic medium of written messages. Many characteristics of the charm make sense in this light: charms frequently have the characters *chih-ling* or *ming* ('to command') at the top (Ch'en 1942: 38; De Groot 1969: VI, 1035); they often contain the expression, 'Let the law

24

3 and 4 Two charms, with translations into ordinary writing along the right-hand side. The left-hand charm (anti-delirium) reads: 'The sun, moon, and all the heavenly bodies, are hereby ordered to restore lucidity to the patient. Let the seven star-gods in the constellation of the Great Bear, and the 36 stellar gods ... relieve him forthwith'. The right-hand charm (for assuaging abdominal pains) reads: 'Powerful as thunder and wind in the present order. Hark! ye maleficent imps. I hereby enjoin that all pains cease forthwith. Signed by ... the god who presides over the thunderbolt'.

be obeyed', a phrase formerly used at the end of official decrees (De Groot 1969: VI, 1951); they are usually written on yellow paper (the imperial color) in ink of cinnabar (the brilliant red used by emperors and officials to mark their writing as authentic and in the custom of *piao p'an*), thus producing the most powerful kind of mandate from the most powerful office in the land (Topley 1953: 63–4; Cormack 1922: 21). A charm, like any official document, must be properly marked with a seal to have validity: 'A charm without a seal is like an army without a commander' (De Groot 1969: VI, 1048).[7] Charms in Taiwan are always marked with the seal of the god from whom their authority derives and sometimes the seal is used alone, as when the clothing of someone whose 'fate needs patching' is stamped.

The fact that charms are often orders is brought out by a portion of a document dictated by the god *Kuan-ti* through spirit writing, and circulated in Hong Kong in 1894 when plague was rife. The god declared:

Those who have sincerely and fervently pledged an oath before me to be virtuous, must draw with my sword thirty-six circles in the air, and below them write this sentence, 'Kwan So-and-so, Assessor for the administration of the labours of the Plague Department, is here'; if affixed to the door, it will prevent all spectres from entering. But woe to you if you thus use my names without repentance of sins or without taking the oath! (De Groot 1969: VI, 1305–6).

In other cases, the orders are less explicitly stated, but the impact the gods' authority is meant to have is clear nonetheless. De Groot describes charms posted in Amoy to protect houses under construction, which experts in charms sold in sets of 12, 8 or 5.

Especially powerful is the set of five, because they represent the authority of the deified rulers of the five parts of the Universe, who, moreover, were the most ancient of sovereigns who introduced the universal Tao among men, thus imparting social order, law, and civilization. The names of those rulers are Fuh-hi, Shen-nung, Hwang-ti, Shao-hao, and Chwen-süh; they are also called the Black, the Blue, the Yellow, the White and the Red Emperor respectively, because the cardinal points correspond with these five colours. These charms, written on yellow or imperial paper, bear the T'ai Kih surrounded by the eight kwa, which is, as we know, a representation of the Universe and its Order; and under this mighty figure stands the impression, in red cinnabar ink, of the seal of the corresponding emperor, thus: 'seal of the Black Emperor', 'seal of the Blue Emperor', etc. (1969: VI, 1058).

In this case, it is not evident that a specific order was being issued. Posting these charms may have been more like showing a name-card from an influential person: whoever saw it might have been hesitant about thwarting one's wishes, since one was evidently so powerfully protected.

In extreme cases, someone with official status might be brought directly into the writing of a charm. In San-hsia I was told that if a corpse is improperly handled, so that the sun and moon are allowed to shine on it, a 'skeleton monster' will be produced. 'Very fierce ones [who will kill people] can only be exorcised

26

by a *Hsiu-tsai* [holder of the "bachelor's" degree, the first rung on the ladder of degrees to governmental office] who writes the orders with a cinnabar pen.' In a similar manner the charms written by gods when they posses a medium are thought to be especially powerful. They are always done on imperial yellow paper, usually written in red ink and marked with a red seal. Sometimes only the *presence* of an official is necessary: 'If an official goes near a place with bad geomantic properties, all the evil spirits and ghosts will leave.' The converse is true as well: I was often told that 'rich men and officials do not fear ghosts' and 'you cannot write charms against a policeman or an official'.

Thus we see that the charm is intended to put bureaucratic machinery into motion: these orders are expected to have an effect on ghostly inhabitants of the world much as another kind of order could be expected to result in a criminal's arrest. This is made explicit in one story I was told:

Once there were two Tans who were very close friends. They even slept in the same bed. One time one of them acquired five dollars — a lot of money in those days — and went to sleep with it in his pocket. When he awoke in the morning it was gone. He knew that his friend must have stolen it, but the friend refused to admit it. Failing to get a confession, he went to the temple of the Taipei city god. There he asked the Taoist priest to write a charm to punish the friend who had stolen the money. But in the meantime the friend had given the money to his wife. She had gone up into the mountains to pick tea, taking the money along. She suddenly felt very sick, and returned home. That night she said that she had heard the sound of handcuffs when she began feeling ill. By the next morning she was dead.

The culprit, deemed guilty because she possessed the stolen goods, was caught up by the god's bureaucratic machinery and taken away, handcuffed, presumably to be punished in the underworld. This machinery is involved in an ordinary death as well. Walshe describes a warrant for the arrest of a dying man sent from the god of the underworld, countersigned by the ancestors and the god of the stove. The dying man may actually see this warrant: 'I saw a man bearing a white thing about six inches long by one inch wide, which he showed me, bearing some characters written on it' (n.d.: 216).

Even when a charm is not submitted especially for the purpose, wrongdoers can be nabbed by spiritual authorities. Doolittle reports that the god of thunder might strike down the unfilial or the wicked and leave a written message justifying his action (1966: II, 301). 'It is a common saying that by the use of a mirror in a particular way, on examining the back of a person struck by thunder, there may often be found characters traced there stating the crime or sin of which he was guilty, and for which he was *"thunderstruck"* ' (p. 302).

Some charms are written in a special code, fully understood only by Taoists or others with special charm-writing skills and the gods themselves (De Groot 1969: VI, 1937, 1939–40).[8] People might well consider this writing 'of a higher order' (perhaps the written correlate of the unintelligible god's speech uttered by mediums) to be effective because it uses a language that belongs exclusively to gods and those close to them. One might think of drawing an analogy between this specialized language and the written language of Chinese officialdom, unintelligible to the illiterate and different in style from the written language ordinary citizens who do read and write are used to. Translated into ordinary language, these charms are also orders, mandates and injunctions. Some of Ch'en Hsiang-ch'un's translations include: 'The Taoist Triad orders that the spirit be killed' (1942: 39); 'I [a god] order verbally the epidemic deity to be in haste to kill the spirit (causing the epidemics of the domestic animals)' (p. 51); 'The Taoist Triad orders the dragon (to eat the malaria-spirit)' (p. 43). The last charm is to be written on yellow paper with a cinnabar writing-brush while a spell is simultaneously recited: 'I (the writer of the charm) received an order from the Very High Lao-chün to command you, the dragon (to eat the malaria-spirit). Do it, speedily, as speedily as to do a work ordered by a legal document!' (p. 40).

It follows sensibly that written charms are posted, like 'no trespassing by order of police' signs, wherever and whenever spirits are feared: outside the house door, especially during epidemics or during construction to pacify earth spirits who may have been disturbed; on pregnant women, especially during slow childbirth to dispel the spirits responsible; in the bedroom of a sick person or on his body to dispel ghosts if they are held responsible; on the sedan-chair or car a bride rides in to keep away dangerous spirits who might threaten her in her vulnerable condition; on the houses in the vicinity of a funeral ceremony to keep the dead man's spirit away (DeGlopper 1974: 64; De Groot 1969: VI, 1957). They can also be burned, transferring them directly to the world of spirits to work their influence there: punishing an unfaithful lover or an unfilial son, making husbands fear their wives, pacifying an angry ancestor, calling a child's soul back. Their effect resides in their ability to act as instructions, on proper authority, to appropriate agents: the god's subordinates are to arrest and detain someone for punishment, the Bed Mother is to help bring a child's soul back.

Even some seemingly arbitrary aspects of the way people deploy charms can be understood as efforts to increase the impact of their message. Ch'en Hsiang-ch'un notes that the charm described above ordering the dragon to eat the malaria spirit can be 'written on a cake and the cake eaten [by the malaria victim] from the bottom to the top' (1942: 39). 'Now, what might be the reason that the present cake should be eaten from the bottom to the top? By eating the cake in this way, the charm written on it will be in a right position in the patient's stomach, otherwise it would be upside down in the stomach' (p. 42). Presumably the charm needs to be right side up in the patient's stomach so that the dragon can read its message properly.

Of course not all charms take their character from bureaucratic communications. Others are intended to strike fear by a literal show of force (a pointed gun as opposed to a 'no trespassing' sign). Spirits fear: knives and swords, especially those used to kill or those made of coins (thought to carry the authority of the monarch who coined them); tigers; mirrors (because their own reflection is frightful); fishnets (because they fear being ensnared) (Doolittle 1966: II, 313; Morgan 1942: 133). And they are repelled by bad smells as when old shoes are burned to ward off the evil spirits who try to snatch away a new-born child's soul (Bredon and Mitrophanow 1927: 122; Cormack 1922: 207). Some charms include both an order and a more literal scare tactic: one I saw in San-hsia had an order for the banishment of ghosts written around a scowling, fearsome face.

I would argue that people use charms, as well as documents in funeral ceremonies and the *chiao*, just as they would use other documents in the world of men: to bring the authority of figures in positions of power to bear on others. In both cases they hope proper authority will be respected, though they also know that, whether because of interference or sheer bravado, it might well not be. Powerful spirits occupy offices and are situated in a chain of command. One might call the efficacy of the actions with which people intend to influence spirits 'bureaucratic efficacy', because it depends on the powers, prerogatives, and constraints that are attached to the spirits' position in the bureaucracy. One can request a pardon from the gods, make a contract with them or banish ghosts on their authority: if the act is done by the proper person, in the proper form, and addressed to a person in an office with the requisite authority, one can reasonably hope for some result.

If the hoped-for effects do not come about, people often blame this on some kind of failure or inability to apply authority, just as we have seen they do in dealing with earthly officials. A ghost might be said to have ignored the orders written on a god's charm or spoken in incantations: some deaths are attributed to ghosts the gods have been unable to expel. A spirit might be said to lack jurisdiction over certain beings: ancestors cannot control ghosts for this reason. A god can be said to be too far above another being to find out why it is causing harm: a family was criticized for calling in *Co-su-kong* (the San-hsia market-town deity) to deal with a ghost because, it was said, *Tho-te-kong*, being a lower-ranked earth god, would be able to communicate with the ghost better. A god may be unable to reverse a decision made in a higher court: if a man's fate (*ming*), determined by the highest god on the basis of his former life, is to die at a certain age, the lower gods 'will have no way of letting him live longer', even though they may want to help.

We can best appreciate the force of this interpretation of the efficacy of charms and other written documents used in ritual if we set it alongside more orthodox interpretations. Recent analysts have commonly referred to portions of Chinese ritual directed to spirits, its paraphernalia, and personnel by specialized terms that set ritual off from ordinary life. We have already come across 'charms'; later we will hear of 'incantations' and 'exorcisms'. In addition, ritual technicians (*fa-shih*) are commonly called 'magicians' (DeGlopper 1974: 48; McCreery 1973: 25)); Taoist ritual words and acts are called 'magic' (Saso 1974: 335–6; 1978: 128); and the official seal of a god is called a 'magic implement'

(Feuchtwang 1977: 602). The authors just mentioned use these terms even though they recognize the resemblance between the form of ritual acts and acts involving earthly officials. The problem is that describing things as 'magical' can imply that they are intended to work in a different way from things involving the everyday bureaucracy.

One example of how 'magical' things might work in a different way is developed in *Notes and Queries in Anthropology*. By their definitions, 'charms' are 'objects invested with magical power'; 'magic' in turn is an act in which 'no appeal is made to spirits' (Committee . . . 1951: 188). The desired end is believed to be achieved directly by the ritual technique itself, i.e., by the use of the appropriate actions, objects, or words. The action, formula, or object is believed to have dynamic power *per se* (p. 187). By this account, 'magic' has its effect in either of two ways:

(a) by contagion, e.g. carrying part of an animal to acquire its characteristics, or as a protection against it; or an object similar in some way to the desired object is carried, kept, or used as a medicament; (b) by association, e.g. some object may be used, or an image may be made and an imitation of the action desired to happen to a third person be performed, spells recited, and charms prepared to bring about desired results (p. 188).

It is possible that describing acts as 'magical' in the sense *Notes and Queries* specifies (or some other) might be justified in certain cases where the ethnographic data show us people do intend their acts to work effects in these special ways. But Chinese written documents used in ritual could not be included among such cases: they are regarded as communications between men and spirits or between spirits with men as intermediaries; they take the form they do and are hoped to have certain effects because, as reports, orders, mandates, injunctions, or notices, they are thought to come before the eyes of beings who will respect the authority of their authors or be favorably impressed by what they describe or request. Returning to the conclusion of Chapter 1, given that the analysis of ritual turns on whether it is interpersonal, and given that Chinese 'charms' and other ritual documents are communications between persons, some of whom are spirits, no analysis of them in terms of 'magical' effects brought about by mechanical or natural causes (to return to Marett, Hart and Honoré), whether the mechanism be 'contagion', 'association' or something else, can possibly convey the sense they have for those who use them.

3

Etiquette and control

In Chapter 2 I argued that some Chinese rituals in which human and non-human persons interact are forms of political activity. Instead of describing these interactions with the specialized vocabulary of 'magic' and like terms, we should describe them in the same terms we would political processes. But perhaps one could protest that I have prejudiced the material in favor of my argument by focusing on written communication in a society where writing was traditionally the preserve of the elite, the vast majority of whom were actively involved in seeking or occupying political office. One might argue that if I had chosen ritual activities less expectedly involved with people exercising political control, I would not be tempted to conclude that Chinese ritual can be seen as an aspect of political control. Perhaps even the close parallels I argued for, between rituals involving human–non-human interaction and ordinary human–human interaction, would disappear.

In this chapter I will look at verbal communication and the exchange or transfer of material goods in ritual activities, items chosen because they are not preeminently or exclusively associated with political processes. My goal is to see whether, even in these areas that are not explicitly political, control – of a more general sort – is still being exercised. My conclusions will be threefold: (1) these aspects of rituals, like the ones discussed earlier, take their form from ordinary life, in this case from the realm of etiquette; (2) one of their central features is the attempt to exercise control (through persuasion based on the communication of deference or compulsion based on knowledge of a system of rules of etiquette); (3) in China those forms of control attempted ritually on non-human persons parallel those forms of control that people regard as effective in ordinary life. Thus even when we move away from explicitly political positions or strata, we find that rituals can still involve the exercise of control over others and that rituals can still be analyzed in the same fashion as interactions in ordinary life.

Being Polite to Spirits and Men

The first ritual means of control I shall discuss involves knowledge of the system of etiquette and the inexorable nature of its moves. People in San-hsia commonly hire ritual experts, Taoist priests, to help with funerals, temple dedications and renewals, the annual ghost festival, and the birthday celebration of their 'host' god, *Co-su-kong*. When I asked ordinary participants in these events why the Taoists were necessary, they often replied that Taoists 'knew how to talk' and consequently could deal with the gods in a more effective manner than others. As one woman said of the Taoists' role in funeral ceremonies: 'The Taoist can speak to the kings of the hells and plead the case of the dead so that he is let through without punishment.' Even some ordinary people are said to be relatively skilled in this way. 'Some people are better able to say things that the gods like to hear and so they are better able to *pai-pai* (pay respect). The gods understand what they are saying better.' One often sees both Taoists and ordinary worshippers making a speech (usually inaudible to bystanders), throwing divining blocks, receiving a negative or ambiguous response, making another speech, and so on, sometimes several times over. As one woman explained,

You keep throwing the blocks until a yes comes up, each time slightly changing what you say. This is because you might have made a mistake in giving your address, or might not have been polite (*kheq-khi*) enough in speaking to the god. One must speak to them as lower generation to higher, using respectful language.

Saying that someone 'knows how to talk to the gods' is the same sort of remark that one makes of a person well-versed in the art of using polite talk in giving compliments, presents, or receiving the same. One says, 'He really knows how to talk.' This implies skill with words and the ability to express respect, but it can also imply such intimate knowledge of the *system* of etiquette that the speaker can get the result he intends literally by *saying the right thing*. Let me illustrate with some examples. In the etiquette of feasting, a host is expected to continually urge his guests to eat, pointing to the various dishes and insisting that each person partake generously. As long as he merely insists by saying, 'Don't be polite', 'Eat more', 'Have some of this', etc., guests are free to play the most polite guest role (one that compromises the host's hospitality), eating very little and only the less expensive dishes. The host's next move might well be to accuse the guests of disliking the food, after which they must protest the contrary and make a show of eating more. The host's final move is to actually place pieces of food on the plates or bowls of his guests, naturally choosing from the finest dishes. They are then compelled to eat whatever he has placed there (or risk giving the host a significant insult), and so allow the host to fulfill his proper role, seeing that guests partake generously of his food.

A similar example comes from the etiquette of greeting bows that existed in the Ch'ing. When host and guest bowed to each other, the host, to be polite, had to see that the guest stood on the most honorable side. But the host had to know what to say to prevent the guest from escaping the honorable position. The missionary, M. Huc, describes this as he saw it practiced during his nineteenth-century travels from western to southern China:

In the provinces of the south of China, the south side is the most honourable; but in the north it is quite the contrary. Of course, the most honourable side is to be offered to the guest: but he, by an ingenious piece of courtesy, may in two words change the state of things, say, *Pe li*, that is, 'We are now observing the ceremony of the north country', which implies, 'I hope that in placing me to the south you are assigning me the least distinguished place.'

But the master of the house politely hastens to frustrate the humble intentions of his guest, by saying *Nan li*, 'Not at all, sir; it is the ceremony of the south, and you are, therefore, in your proper place.' Sometimes the visitor himself affects to take the least honourable, but then the host excuses himself saying, 'I should not dare'; and, passing before his guest, taking care not to turn his back on him, he proceeds to his proper position, a little behind (1970: I, 209–10).

Walshe gives us a final example which arises out of a host's attempt to seat his guests at the dinner table in positions of relative rank:

If the person, who is manifestly best entitled to sit in the highest seat, persists in declining the honour, the host will be put to considerable inconvenience. A useful method of avoiding such difficulties obtains on occasions of particular importance, and is as follows:

The host stands at the chief seat, and, holding up the winepot in his hand, calls out, 'Brother So-and-So': he then pours out a cup of wine, and, putting down the wine vessel, makes a respectful bow ... The guest replies with a similar gesture, and is compelled to accept the seat thus allotted to him; the other seats are appropriated in the same manner. Sometimes the guests will attempt to remonstrate, but no serious effort is made to refuse the seats thus arranged (n.d.: 94).

I would suggest that in the view of ordinary people, the ability Taoists have as, to a lesser extent, do others who 'know how to *pai-pai*' is of this order. As respectful hosts inviting the gods to come, or as petitioners asking a favor, they know the requisite moves in the system of interactions to compel the gods to behave as they wish.[1]

But being polite in the ordinary world, as in the world of spirits, consists in far more than knowing how to compel others using the rules of etiquette. It consists, in large part, in knowing how to communicate respect and deference adequately; in Taiwanese terms, one shows respect (*chieng*) to others by deferring (*niu:*) to them. As we will see, this, no less than the more overt compulsion just discussed, can get other beings to behave as one wishes. At the least, communicating that one is respectful or deferential can avoid offending another person or spirit and remove one potential reason he might refuse a request. At the most, communicating that one is respectful or deferential can flatter the other person or spirit and so help persuade him to act on one's behalf, especially if one also communicates confidence in the other person's or spirit's ability at the same time.

In communicating with other persons verbally, it is often important to know how to address them.[2] This is true among kinsmen: in Taiwan children are taught early on what to call the many kinsmen around them: new daughters-in-law are introduced to their husband's kinsmen by the phrase 'You call him "brother" [or some such]'; people discuss the coming visit of a distant kinsman at length, concerned about how each person should properly address him. Aside from kinsmen, a title plus surname usually suffices for those one does not know well or for one's superiors: 'Mr' (*Sian-si:*) 'Mrs' (*Thai-thai*) 'Miss' (*Siou-cia*), 'Medical Doctor' (*I-sieng*), 'Ph.D.' (*Po-shih*) or 'Mayor' (*Chen-chang*). If one does not know another person's surname, there are polite formulas one can use to elicit it.

It is safe to say that the decision about what form of address to use is often (though it need not be) motivated by a desire to influence the other person's response. One can avoid offending, and attempt persuading, by using a respectful form of address that expresses deference toward the other person. Skill in using form of address to affect another person's response depends partly on judgement (when a particular form will have a particular result) and partly on knowledge. Just as one must know the system of etiquette to fulfill the polite host role, one must know the polite formulae by which one can elicit another person's surname or given name (Kiong 1906: 52).

Address forms for the gods can be put to the same purposes as address forms for men. In San-hsia, the temples everyone frequents pose no problem; *Co-su-kong* and *Tho-te-kong* can be addressed by the same names people use to refer to them. But visiting a temple for the first time can be bewildering. The array of gods' images on the altar is often overwhelming, and there is no easy way to tell which is the host god or what his or her name is. Even the literate would often be hard put to make out the god's name written on a ribbon around his neck, given that the image may be encased in glass and many feet away in a dark, smoky hall. When I accompanied an elderly woman to visit a medium (*tang-ki*) in San-hsia, she was obviously at a loss about how to address her query to the more than twelve images on the *tang-ki*'s altar. The *tang-ki*'s assistant informed her: 'Address them "*chieng-sin*" (true gods).' There is the further problem that a god may have more than one name, or a short name and a long name. '*Co-su-kong*' is a shortened version of '*Chieng-cui Co-su*'; '*Ang-kong*' (Honorable Gentlemen) is a common name for two deities who visit San-hsia every year, but some people say their proper names are 'Protector Physician' and 'Protector King'. Knowing the gods' proper names plays a role in the effectiveness of one's prayer. Just as one's great uncle or mayor might be offended if one addressed him incorrectly, so might the gods. Hence people are usually careful to ask a temple-keeper or fellow petitioner how to address a god when they are unsure.

Taoist priests and lay ritual experts have sure knowledge of how to address the gods. At times Taoists invite the gods' presence primarily by calling their names, and lay villagers regarded as ritual experts may read long lists of gods' names to summon them to mediumistic sessions.[3] It is in the sense that these lists of names address the gods properly — and hence politely — that they serve as 'incantations' summoning the gods' presence. As among men, knowledge of the correct form of address can be used to obtain a desired response.

Beyond the form of address, the substance of verbal communications may also communicate respect or deference. A host, always deferential to his guests for the occasion at least, prefaces his requests with the polite 'please', '*chia:*'; and deprecates his house, food, table, and wife as being unworthy of his honored guests. Aside from self-effacive language, making a substantial request is itself a form of flattery, for it implies that the person asked has the ability to grant it. A western businessman notes

the peculiar courtesy with which every request for favors must be treated. No request appears to be improper. The more impossible it is to grant (according to Western standards) the more honor it confers on the person of whom it is made; it seems to ascribe to him powers above the ordinary (Baker 1928: 426).

As for the gods, we have seen above that Taoist written communications to the gods include both self-effacive language and elaborate praise of the spirits' abilities. (See pp. 23–4.) The same is true of the spoken invocations used in spirit-medium temples in Singapore:

Respectfully we invite the presence of the Great Saint equal with Heaven . . . We, your followers, worshipping the Great Saint equal with Heaven, beseech you to descend speedily, for we know that when the order is given the Heavenly Army will come to our aid as quickly as we hope . . . Your voice like thunder makes the *shen* and devils tremble. With your golden bar you have great strength, chasing the devils and whipping evil spirits. You can save a myriad of people. Now we invite you, the one who can shake Heaven, to come before this altar. With your sword you can kill evil spirits, and in this way you can demonstrate your spiritual powers. Wake, wake and save us (Elliott 1955: 170).

Illustrating these points further, Eitel gives a detailed description of the verbal and gestural ways deference and flattery are communicated to a god invited to write in sand with a special implement, for the obvious purpose of pleasing him and so obtaining his cooperation:

Two or three of the company assembled go to the door, burn there some gold paper and make then an indefinite number of bows and prostrations, receiving as it were the spirit on entering the house. Having conducted him into the hall, an arm-chair is moved to the table while incense and candles are lighted. At the same time the medium approaches, the handle of the magic pencil resting on the palms of both hands, but so that the end of the twig touches the surface of the table strewn with sand. He places his outspread hands near the head of the table and addressing the spirit with becoming reverence says: 'Great spirit, if you have arrived, be pleased to write the character (arrived) on this table.' Immediately the magic pencil begins to move and the required character appears legibly written in the sand whereupon all assembled request the spirit to sit down on the large arm-chair, whilst the Deity, that is supposed to have conducted him hither, is likewise politely asked to sit down on another chair. The whole company now bow and prostrate themselves before the seats of both spirits, and some pour out wine and burn gold paper . . . When a sentence is finished . . . the sand on the table has to be smoothed again with a bamboo roller, and whilst this is being done the whole company address flattering speeches to the spirit, praising his poetical talents, to which the magic pencil replies by writing on the table the characters (it's ridiculous). If any one present behaves improperly, displaying a want of reverence, the spirit writes down some sentences containing a sharp rebuke . . . In this way conversation is kept up without flagging until midnight (when the male principle begins to be active). Then the spirit breaks off the conversation and addressing the whole company writes on the table: 'Gentlemen, I am very obliged for your liberal presents but now I must beg leave to depart.' To this all persons present reply saying: 'Please, great spirit, stop a little longer', but the spirit jots down as if in great hurry the two characters (excuse me, I am off). Then all assembled say, 'If there was any want of respect or attention, great spirit, we beseech thee forgive us this sin.' All walk then to the house-door burning gold paper and there take leave of the spirit with many bows and prostrations (Eitel 1867: 164—5).

In this case, the god (superior in status to his petitioners) generously expresses polite deference to them and they respond by showing even greater deference. In other cases, superiors may omit deference from their behavior and speech, exposing simply their authority. This can be seen clearly when Taoists act as delegates of powerful gods, and on their behalf demand that evil (and lower) spirits suffer a certain fate. In Michael Saso's account of a Red-head Taoist's rite for curing a child's illness, the priest first summons the various spirits at his behest, writes a charm, seals it, and says:

> I command the source of all pains in the body —
> Muscle pains, headaches, eye sores, mouth sores
> Aching hands and aching feet
> ([insert the particular ailment of the child]) —
> With the use of this magic of mine,
> Here before this Taoist altar,
> May all demons be bound and captured,
> May they be cast back into Hell's depths.
> 'Ch'iu-ch'iu Chieh-chieh'
> You are sent back to your source!
> Quickly, Quickly, obey my command! (1974: 329).

He then consults the gods through divination to see whether the proper spirit has been banished.

As in the case of written documents, the priest is exercising authority delegated from gods much as officials in the earthly bureaucracy exercised authority delegated from the emperor. The priest's commands have force, and will be heeded (if they are) because of the powers that stand behind them. In this setting, respect and deference have no place. They are lacking too in another 'exorcism', described by John Henry Gray. The priest cries:

'Gods of heaven and earth, invest me with the heaving seal, in order that I may eject from this dwelling-house all kinds of evil spirits. Should any disobey me, give me power to deliver them for safe custody to the rulers of such demons.' Having received the authority for which he prayed, he calls to the evil spirit —

'As quick as lightning, depart from this dwelling.' He then takes a bunch of willows which he dips into the cup, and with which he besprinkles the east, west, north, and south corners of the house. Laying it down and taking up the sword again, and still carrying the cup in his left hand, he now goes to the east corner of the house and exclaims, 'I have the authority', – 'Tai-Shaong–Loo–Kwaa.' When he has said this, he fills his mouth with the water of exorcism, which he immediately ejects upon the eastern wall. He then calls aloud, 'Kill the green evil spirits which come from unlucky stars, or let them be driven far away' (1878: II, 18–19).

When ordinary people address low spirits, the language they use also lacks expressions of deference. In San-hsia the offerings left to ghosts after a funeral are presented to them with these words; 'Hoo-oo, come and eat': one does not know who they are, so one cannot address them; one does not respect them (any more than one does a beggar) so one cannot express deference to them; one does not have authority over them, so one cannot order them about. Consequently they are simply notified that they should come and eat.

Transfer or Exchange of Goods

As in preceding sections, I will construct comparisons between exchange or transfer of goods among men on the one hand and between spirits and men on the other. My main objective is to discuss ways in which exchange of goods can be used to exert control, but I should note that not all exchanges play this role. Some are simply intended to maintain an existing relationship. For example, in Taiwan, the amount received in red envelopes (*ang-pau*) from those who attend a wedding or white envelopes from those who attend a funeral is carefully recorded so that, when the occasion demands, a return in like amount can be made. 'You have to consider the last *ang-pau* you received and return about the same amount.' Similarly, some parts of wedding ceremonies involve an exchange of goods balanced in value: if the groom's family sends 'six kinds' of goods at the engagement ceremony, the bride's family must return 'six kinds' with the dowry. The only other alternative is that the number of kinds is doubled, 'twelve kinds' being sent and returned.

In another example, Doolittle tells us that when a friend or relative is about to set off on a journey – to engage in business or be a mandarin in another town – one presents 'vegetables for the road', gifts for the journey. Upon his return home, the traveller has to present gifts to these friends and relatives 'having due regard to the comparative value and quantity of presents proffered him as "vegetables for the road" when he left home. Unless one should thus remember his relatives and friends on his return, he would be regarded as destitute or ignorant of politeness' (1966: II, 236). Walshe quotes the Book of Rites: 'Presents should come and go; those which go only, and do not come [i.e. are not returned], are not "in order", and those which come only and do not go are not "in order".' He says that there is only one exception to this: when a friend or relative suffers a loss of property from fire, one sends presents of household goods. None of these can ever be returned, nor can one send a return gift or even a word of thanks, for this would imply a return obligation, and with it the wish that the donor's house would burn down (n.d.: 165–6).

In other cases, a balance is kept between material objects and a service of some kind, also to maintain or fulfill the expectations that go along with an existing relationship. Within the Ch'ing bureaucracy a magistrate newly arrived in a district would expect presents from all who ranked below him. 'He expects a present graduated in value according to the comparative lucrativeness of the stations which the officers fill. The amount from each is fixed by custom. Unless they should give it on the arrival of the mandarin, professedly as an expression of their satisfaction and respect, but really in order to ingratiate themselves in his good will, matters would not go smoothly with them. They would be frequently faulted and required to do their work over again, etc.' (Doolittle 1966: I, 321).

In contrast to the above cases, people sometimes attempt to get something out of a transfer of goods aside from the continuation of an existing relationship. For example, sending goods in excess of what is expected can be a way of demonstrating great resources, and perhaps relatively high status. Doolittle describes gifts offered for show, which were not intended to be kept: they were called 'horses to look at' (1966: II, 235). Sometimes items were only rented or borrowed until it was certain which would be kept, and sometimes only an order for certain goods from a shop was presented, an order that would only be filled if the recipient in fact retained the goods (1966: II, 235). Just as sending many gifts can demonstrate great resources and status, so also can refusing all or a large portion of gifts one is offered. As Kiong describes it, when a moderate number of gifts is sent, for example four or eight, one should accept about half; when a large number is sent, for example twenty or thirty, one should only accept about one third or one fourth (1906: 62).

The logic of demonstrating status by giving excessively and refusing excessively informs Taiwanese engagement fees: the groom's family sends a 'large deposit' and a 'small deposit', each in cash, in two separate stacks. (In one engagement in 1969 the large deposit was NT\$32,000 and the small one was NT\$22,000.)[4] Like Doolittle's 'horses to look at', the 'large deposit' is often borrowed. The bride's family must then decide which to accept. In almost all cases they take the small amount. This allows them both to defray the cost of the dowry somewhat and to demonstrate their own resources by refusing the larger amount. Some very wealthy families (mindful of status and heedless of profit) have been known to refuse both and some very greedy ones (heedless of status and mindful of profit) have been known to take the larger amount.

The most obvious way people use the transfer of goods to accomplish a goal other than the maintenance of a relationship, is to offer a gift to someone, hoping he or she will provide some special, out of the ordinary favor. A common pattern seems to be to make a token payment when the request is made, to show respect, and then follow it by a substantial gift when the desired object or service is in hand. Walshe recommends that those who wish for help in obtaining a house to rent should call on the local notable, taking some suitable present of food. After quarters are secured, he should give a feast for the community, sending a special set of dishes to the notable (n.d.: 129, 132). At other times one might make an extraordinary gesture in advance, with a mind to a petition to be put forward in the future (Doolittle 1966: I, 322).

When we turn to the spirits, many of the same ways of maintaining relationships, demonstrating status, or exercising control are evident. Food offerings, given on gods' birthdays or on certain festivals, are intended to maintain existing relationships with the gods. People in San-hsia said a relationship (*ong-lai*, literally, going and coming) with a god is created in part by people and things going and coming. One pays courtesy calls on friends, superiors, and the gods, taking along a gift (and also using a form of address, manner of speech, and body posture) appropriate to their status. 'We think of taking presents when we worship in the same way we think of taking presents when we visit a friend.' The return hoped for can be goods (crops, sons, or money) or services (preservation of health or family harmony).

Among men we have seen that one can offer or refuse gifts in excess of the minimum necessary to maintain a relationship, in order to make a statement about how great one's resources are. Great resources often go along with high status, so it should be no surprise that high-ranking spirits are thought to have such great resources that they can leave human offerings untouched. They are offered food, ritual money, incense, and wine. But many people say the high gods do not really need these things: like the 'horses to look at' or the 'large deposit', the food offerings are returned and eventually consumed by the donors and their guests. The point seems to be that the high gods enjoy the resources and privileges of a wealthy, powerful class: whatever humans offer could only be pitifully below their standard of luxury. Low-ranking ghosts, in contrast, really are in need of sustenance. Perhaps this is why offerings to them either are left on the ground or, though eaten, are said to 'have no flavor'. Ghosts, like most ordinary people, cannot afford the polite niceties of returning a gift untouched. In this respect, ghosts resemble low-level officials, who accept gifts for special favors to local people. One woman told me the difference between food offerings to the gods and money packets given to local police is that one can bring the god's offerings home and eat them, but one never sees the money packets again.

In the case of ritual money too, high gods do not need what people offer. A man told Arthur Wolf, ' "Money" offered to the gods is not money at all, but is more "like the petitions people sent to the government". He scoffed at the idea that the gods would be interested in money' (1974a: 181). In contrast again, ghosts and lower gods are assumed to need particular amounts. The exact amount of ritual money burnt to encourage ghosts to leave is often specified in the god's instructions. In one case *Co-su-kong* instructed that twenty-five sheets of a certain type of ritual money, said to be worth the equivalent of NT$10,000 each. were to be burned for a ghost. And at funeral ceremonies, an actor personifying *Tho-te-kong*, one of the lowest gods in the hierarchy, haggles, insisting on more and more (actual) money before he will agree to lead the deceased to the underworld. The ancestors also care about particular amounts of money and food, and for this reason more than one detailed report is read to them at funerals (i.e. the *ce-bun*).[5]

Just as among men, when the need arises, one can make a special request of the gods, accompanying it by a token offering, promising a great deal more if the request is granted (Doolittle 1966: I, 145–6, 155). In Taiwan these are called *'hi-guan'* (pledges). The item promised can be a special whole pig, a *Ti-kong*; an opera performance (which gods enjoy as much as men); a meritorious act such as following in one of the god's processions, or more simply, ordinary fruit or meat offerings. Making good on the pledge is called *'huan-guan'* (returning the pledge). Alternatively, just as in ordinary life, one can store up credit by performing meritorious acts in advance of any need.

If the request is not granted, no pledge need be returned (Doolittle 1966: I, 162–3), but one continues to express respect to the god despite this. Doolittle notes that an 'arrow' bearing the character 'command' may be borrowed from the temple of a particular idol to dispel sickness. If the sick person recovers, a thank offering is returned to the temple with the arrow. If the sick person dies, the arrow is returned with a simple offering of ritual money, incense, and candles. 'These are not to be regarded as a *thank*-offering, but only as tokens of respect, without which, the divinity would be offended' (1966: I, 145–6).

In sum, we see that, even when we attend to forms of action not exclusively found among political elites in Chinese society, rituals involving the gods will utilize some of the same forms of control that are regarded as effective among men: compulsion through manipulation of the system of etiquette; flattery through verbal and gestural forms of deference, demonstration of status through display of wealth, and use of wealth as payment for desired favors. As with the analysis of written communications in Chinese ritual, a by-product of realizing that people attempt to control spirits in the same way they attempt to control other people is that the specialized vocabulary for use with spirits can be abandoned: incantations and exorcisms become aspects of either verbal etiquette or the prerogatives of rank; offerings become goods due to status superiors. These conclusions are limited to the forms of interaction between men and spirits. It does not follow necessarily that the system of authority that is believed to exist in the spirit world mirrors exactly the one that actually exists among men. This matter will be taken up in Part III.

The enterprise of Part I can be restated in terms of an image devised by Friedrich Waismann for language:

Etiquette and control

One feels a marked difference when one compares such statements as: a material object statement, a sense-datum statement, a law of nature, a geometrical proposition, a statement describing national characteristics, a statement describing a half-faded memory picture, a statement describing a dream, a proverb, and so forth. It is as if each of these statements was constructed in a different *logical style* . . . We may set ourselves the task of grouping statements of our language according to the similarity of their usage in distinct domains, in *language-strata* as I shall venture to call them. Thus laws will form one language stratum, material object statements another one, sense datum statements yet another one, and so on (1965a: 235).

Waismann, following Ludwig Wittgenstein's lead, was concerned to illuminate the differences among strata, pointing for example to variation in how precise concepts are or to variation in what kinds of 'logic' (laws of inference) operate. 'Looking upon a logic as a characteristic which sets its stamp upon a particular language stratum' allows us to recognize precise concepts and the law of excluded middle in the language stratum of mathematics, but not be blinded to open texture in the stratum of half-faded memory pictures or contradiction in the stratum of aphorisms (p. 238). My purpose has been to consider two strata of Chinese language and action that anthropologists have frequently assumed operate according to different 'logics' — politics and 'magical' acts. My whole point is that the same logic informs them both: it is as important to spot unexpectedly similar logic in seemingly separate strata as it is to differentiate the logic of genuinely separate strata.

PART II

Codes

4

Divination

There is no general term in Chinese that describes the class of all the divinatory methods I shall discuss; rather there are separate verbs and objects for nearly every sort. They seem to naturally fall together, however, because they resemble each other in a vague way, and are characterized by an overlapping series of traits: they are efforts to obtain information about the past, present, or future, with regard to one's self or others, by recourse to experts with superior or specialized knowledge or to handbooks containing such knowledge. For reasons of space, rather than principle, I will not include a detailed examination of efforts to obtain medical advice from Chinese-style or western-style doctors.

My first task is to separate divinatory acts that involve interpersonal trans-actions from those that involve causal or other connections. One set of divinatory methods should be described as interpersonal in the sense that they are explicitly understood as efforts to communicate with the gods. Another set of methods do not involve forms of communication between sentient beings as a central feature: instead they are concerned with understanding forces and processes that operate in the world. I will begin by describing a range of practices I witnessed in northern Taiwan that are communicative acts and then move to a range of practices that are not, introducing descriptions of these practices from elsewhere in China in a limited way.

Perhaps the most ubiquitous form of interpersonal divination in Taiwan involves the use of two crescent-shaped blocks, round on one side, flat on the other, called *pue* (Mandarin *pei*). They are held with their flat sides together and raised in the direction of the god's or ancestors' altar. A question or petition is murmured and then the *pue* are dropped (*puaq*) onto the floor. The way they fall (both flat sides up; both flat sides down; one up, one down) constitutes the god's answer: 'laughing', 'no' or 'yes', respectively.

The person who wishes to make inquiries of any particular god or goddess kneels down before the image, or whatever represents it, and bows his head reverently toward the ground several times while on his knees. He then proceeds to state his circumstances or his plans, presenting his request, and begging an intimation of the will of the divinity, or the condition of things in the future in regard to his case. He then rises to his feet, and, taking the kà-pue, with its plain surfaces placed together, passes it through the smoke of the burning incense, with a circular motion, a few times. He then throws it up reverently before the idol. The nature of the answer is supposed to be determined by the relative position of the pieces as they lie on the ground. If the flat surface of one falls upward, and the flat surface of the other falls downward, the answer is regarded as affirmative, or favorable. If both oval surfaces fall upward, the answer is negative, or unfavorable. If they both fall downward, the answer is indifferent, neither very good nor very bad (Doolittle 1966: II, 107—8).

There are numerous conventions governing how more than one fall should be read in combination. Sometimes people say a prayer, drop the blocks, then unless they fall as a 'yes' say another prayer of a slightly different form, drop them again, and so on until a favorable response is obtained. In one case I saw, when elaborate offerings had been made to the gods on the occasion of an old woman's birthday, the Taoist priest prayed and cast the blocks over and over but obtained no affirmative response. There were worried looks around the room and whispered consultations about whether the priest had correctly communicated all the information about the offerings and the family presenting them. But when a 'yes' finally came up, a spontaneous murmur of 'It's all right' went around the room.

Sometimes the blocks are cast only once, especially if a logical reason for the first response presents itself. One family made offerings to an ancestor on her death-day anniversary, presenting them in the family's own home for the first time, instead of in the ancestral hall. When the blocks came up 'laughing' it was said — 'The ancestor is amused to be eating in this house for the first time' — and left at that.

At other times multiple casts are significant. A common pattern in San-hsia is to make a maximum of three casts. If one of the three comes up affirmative, the answer is 'yes'. Otherwise it is 'no'. D.H. Kulp details a more complex code.

The woman who earnestly wishes for something comes to the temple, lights incense and places a few sticks in each receptacle set up for that purpose. This done, she sees that the lamps are lighted, but first she will make her offering of money. She then goes to the long bench and, kneeling, takes up the *bei* [*pei*], holds them together in her two hands, lifts them up and down before her, and bows to the god, saying,

Chiu Lao Ye, gong wuh loh yü. Ts chi shen bei. (Pray God, let it not rain. Grant favorable omens!)

Then she throws the *bei* on the dirt floor of the temple and notes how they fall. She should throw three times in all. If they fall in favoring combinations she is satisfied and goes out. Otherwise she may continue until luck breaks and the omens favor her. Sometimes she retires in sorrow when no favorable throw comes.

The combinations are as follows:

1. Smooth and round is *shen bei* and means the gods are favorable.
2. Smooth and smooth is *siao* [*hsiao*] *bei* and means the gods laugh at the prayer.

3. Round and round is *wen bei* and means the gods refuse to speak one
way or the other.

The worshippers always ask for *shen bei* but *shen bei* does not always come.
That is why they throw three times. The chances for a successful combination
are greater than in one throw. Gambling with the gods to win the heart's desire
is no matter of fun.

In three throws, 1−1−3 means the prayer will be granted surely. This is the
most favorable combination of any three throws. 3−3−1 would not count, so
the throws would be repeated. The second best omen is the combination 1−1−1.
1−3−3 means the answer might be favorable and involves repeated throws. The
following combinations mean unfavorable omens: 1−2−2, 1−2−1, 3−2−1,
and 3−3−3.

A worshipper was asked what she does when the omen do not come
favorably the first three throws. She replied: 'Keep on throwing' (1925: 296−
7).

Partly because *pue* are such simple objects, they are ubiquitous. They are
found wherever there is an image, picture, or incense pot of a god or ancestor,
be it in a city temple or a village household. In contrast, divination by 'asking for
a lot' (*thiu-chiam*) requires a more complex apparatus: many small *Tho-te-kong*
temples do not have lots; most major temples do. Having this system is one indication that a god has a reputation for responding to requests effectively (being
lieng). There are three elements in this communicative system: a pair of *pue*; a
set of numbered lots (usually 100 long thin strips of bamboo) held upright in a
large bamboo tube; and a set of slips of paper, each bearing a message, numbered to correspond to the set of lots.

To ask for a lot, one first identifies oneself before the deity and states what
general topic one wishes information about. The topic one states must be
chosen from a list limited by convention including such things as 'marriage',
'pregnancy', 'litigation', 'search for wealth', or 'fame'. One then drops the *pue*
to see whether the god is willing to provide information on this topic. If one
obtains a 'yes' *pue*, one chooses a lot at random from the container (which
conceals the numbers on the sticks) and drops the *pue* again. If they do not
come up 'yes', one chooses other lots one by one, dropping the *pue* for each until
the god indicates one has picked the correct lot by giving a 'yes' *pue*. One then
obtains the paper slip corresponding to this lot from pigeonholes accessible to
anyone or, for a small charge, from a temple-keeper or priest behind a counter.

On the top or right side of the paper slip there is usually a stanza of verse or
a brief passage from a historical work; alongside or below this there is usually a
translation of the general message in particular terms. The translation can be
brief. Sometimes, only the conventional list of topics is printed with a brief bit
of information after each one: 'Marriage: unharmonious; pregnancy: bear a son;
litigation: will receive justice' and so on. If one can read the message and understand it to one's satisfaction, there is no more to be done. Otherwise one can
consult the keeper or priest who, perhaps with the aid of a handbook, will offer
further interpretation.[1] As Doolittle describes it,

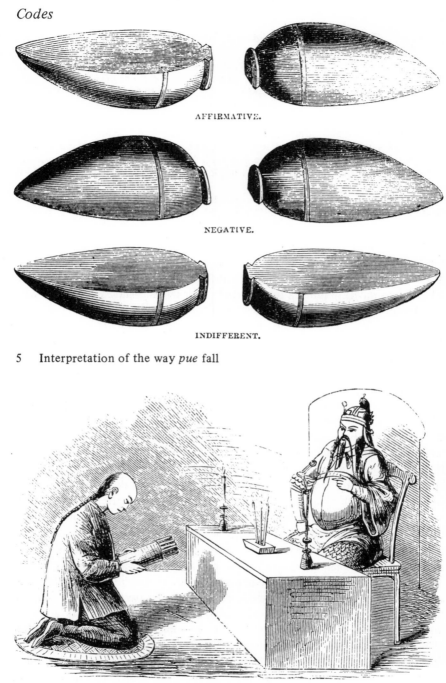

AFFIRMATIVE.

NEGATIVE.

INDIFFERENT.

5 Interpretation of the way *pue* fall

CASTING LOTS.

6 Shaking out a *chiam* in front of the image of a god

Some of the stanzas have an explanation attached which is designed to aid the applicant in understanding and applying them. Most frequently, however, he is left to make his own application and inference after an examination of its general sentiments, or its allusions to historic personages or events (1966: II, 110).

Other means of getting information from the gods require consultation of an expert. On the streets of San-hsia one can seek out an itinerant diviner who uses a pair of trained birds in 'bird biting lots'. Each of the birds pecks out a stick from a set of eight marked with characters and two cards from a set of sixty-four depicting well-known legends. Using the information on the sticks and cards the diviner speaks to the question the client presents. Sometimes the interpretation seems to be obvious: the character *ong* (king) drawn on a stick means one will have authority over others. But at other times, the diviner gives an interpretation based on his secret knowledge of this divinatory system. In any case, the gods govern the choice of particular sticks and cards: the diviner told me that before leaving for the day's work he presents the birds to the goddess *Kuan-im*, telling her that he is going to tell fortunes. Then, when the birds pull out the cards and sticks, the goddess's spirit is with them, directing what they do.[2]

Or one can visit the *Ma-co* temple in San-hsia, where the temple-keeper divines by means of a tortoise shell and three coins. As in the preceding cases, this method involves communication with a deity, here the goddess *Ma-co*. The keeper burns incense for her and describes the petitioner's problem to her. Then he places three coins in the tortoise shell and shakes them until they bounce out, landing, according to the goddess's will, heads or tails. On the basis of a series of such falls, the keeper consults his handbooks and deciphers *Ma-co*'s message.[3]

Because all these sorts of divination are basically means of communicating with the gods, they irresistibly merge into more complete forms of communication with them: 'asking the gods' (*mng-sin*), during which the gods write or verbalize a direct response, having possessed a person or implement for that purpose. Numerous descriptions of these practices exist in the literature, so I will be brief.[4] In Ch'inan a god is often beseeched to possess men who stand and wait while supporting the two poles of the god's sedan chair. Signs of possession are rhythmic jumping and heavy breathing. After possession, one long pole supporting the chair is extended forward and whichever man is possessed by the god's spirit uses it to write characters (sometimes in sand or sawdust) on a table top. Needless to say, interpretation of the amorphous markings he makes is rather difficult. All those who can read crowd around the table and make guesses. The god signals a correct guess by slamming the chair pole down onto the table once, an incorrect guess by slamming it down twice. The god may also use the man's body to get the message across: adopting postures signifying pleasure or anger, shaking or nodding the head, going to fetch something himself, or leading the group to a particular place. In other cases the god communicates by possessing the writing-implement itself. A charm is burnt, designed to cause the god to descend, enter the pen, and deliver its oracle in writing. If he does not soon indicate his presence, another charm is burnt. His presence is manifested by a slow movement of the point of the pen, tracing characters in the sand. After writing a line or two on the sand, the pen ceases to move, and the characters are transferred to paper. After this, if the response is unfinished, another line is written, and so on until the pen entirely ceases its motion, which signifies that the spirit of the divinity has taken its departure from the pen (Doolittle 1966: II, 114).

The most complete, potentially least ambiguous form of communication is when the god actually speaks through a man.[5] People said that most *tang-ki* (mediums) can only let the characters written in the sand illustrate the god's meaning. A few are able to talk and 'directly make known the god's instructions'. Most professional *tang-ki* that people consult in the market town or city purport to speak the god's words, though people often question whether they are genuinely possessed.[6]

In sharp contrast to the sorts of divination we have discussed so far, we find a whole range of other sorts that do not include interaction with sentient beings. Consider, for example, geomancy, the system of computation of forces and configurations in the earth and air that bears upon the siting of graves and buildings. The geomancer *calculates* the degree and extent of forces in the environment that bear upon the site (breaths, dragon forces, etc.); he *measures* the axis of the object to be sited as well as of surrounding features of the landscape using a magnetic compass; he *classifies* surrounding hills and hollows according to their shapes; he *correlates* facts about the site with the environment. He does not send nor does he receive messages from sentient beings.[7] In Stephan Feuchtwang's words, geomancy is not to be associated with

divination which reads anything believed to be communicated by gods or the souls of dead kin or friends through oracles, dreams, signs and omens. The *Feng-shui hsien-sheng* [geomancer] is not reporting from an other-worldly vantage point. He is only reading signs in the sense of being able to tell by superior knowledge from outward appearance what is the state of certain profound and far-reaching processes behind them (1974a: 201).

Similarly, no form of horoscopic divination based on the eight characters that describe the year, month, day, and hour of one's birth need involve any communication with spirit beings. One merely presents accurate information about one's own birth (or, in addition, about that of one's prospective spouse) to an expert in such matters who performs calculations, often using handbooks which, in Doolittle's words, 'teach how to prognosticate by a reference to the precise time of one's birth, compared with the five elements, deducing a conclusion propitious or unpropitious' (1966: II, 332). One can also perform simple calculations oneself using an ordinary almanac. The Taiwan almanac of 1975 has one chart showing what years of birth are compatible for marriage, and another correlating the sum of numbers representing the year, month, day, and hour of one's birth with fortunes. Given the relevant assumptions about the consequences that follow from correspondences between the time of birth, the cycle of the five elements, the position of the stars, and so on, these are calculations about the natural course of events. They are no different in spirit from weather forecasting or our calculations of when a baby will be born by subtracting three months from the first day of the woman's last menstrual period and adding seven days.

Two other forms of divination not generally available in the San-hsia area are described for other parts of China. Inspection of the physiognomy is clearly based on calculations, much as geomancy and horoscopic divination are:

This kind of fortune-tellers do not open a shop, but usually select a convenient place in the street, where they can display a chart, to which they make frequent reference. They inspect the eyes and eyebrows, nose, mouth, ears, cheek-bones and temples, the lips, teeth, and the beard or whiskers of the customer, if a man. They compare the 'five governors' together (ears, eyes, nose, mouth, and eyebrows) to determine whether they agree or are fitting, and whether the expression of countenance is proper and correct, and whether it is honorable or mean. They observe the manner of one's walking or sitting, and draw inferences in regard to the future fortunes of the individual, whether he will be rich or poor, an officer or a beggar. They dilate on the revelations of the physiognomy as relating to the past good or bad fortunes of the dupe, or to his future good or bad fortunes (Doolittle 1966: II, 332—3).

The analysis of written characters resembles our analysis of handwriting or doodles: something in the client's personal situation leads him to write a character, which is then analyzed, or, in some cases, to choose a character from a selection provided by the diviner (Doolittle 1966: II, 335; DeGroot 1890: 239). Williams describes the diviner himself making the selection, presumably on the client's behalf:

The fortune-tellers also consult fate by means of bamboo slips bearing certain characters, as the sixty-four diagrams, titles of poetical responses, or lists of names, etc. The applicant comes up to the table and states his desire; he wishes to know whether it will be fair weather, which of a dozen doctors shall be selected to cure his child, what sex an unborn infant will be, where his stolen property is, or any other matter. Selecting a slip, the diviner dissects the character into its component parts, or in some other way, and writes the parts upon a board lying before him, joining to them the time, the names of the person, five planets, colors, viscera, and other heterogeneous things, and from them all, putting on a most cabalistic, sapient look, educes a sentence which contains the required answer. The man receives it as confidently as if he had entered the sybil's cave and heard her voice, pays his fee, and goes away. Others, less shrewd, refer to books in which the required answer is contained in a sort of equivocal delphian distich (Williams 1965: II, 261).

In these two cases as well, no communication with sentient beings is involved.

At this point we can begin to identify the differences between the sorts of divination that involve interpersonal transaction and the sorts that do not.

To begin, consider the nature of the devices used in each sort of divination. It is obvious that the pen or pole used in 'asking the gods' functions as a writing-

A PHYSIOGNOMIST.

FORTUNE-TELLING BY MEANS OF WORDS.

7 and 8   Two kinds of divination

52

implement. It should be no less obvious that the blocks, sticks, coins, and cards used in *puaq-pue, thiu-chiam*, tortoise shell, and bird divination are also tools of communication. The gods use them, manipulate them, to give answers or advice. The pattern in which they fall (or the ones selected) are treated as words or sentences 'uttered' by the god. They are speech acts. Consequently people try to decipher them. As Searle has said of Mayan hieroglyphs,

It is a logical presupposition . . . of current attempts to decipher the Mayan hiero- glyphs that we at least hypothesize that the marks we see on the stones were produced by beings more or less like ourselves and produced with certain kinds of intentions. If we were certain the marks were a consequence of, say, water erosion, then the question of deciphering them or even calling them hieroglyphs could not arise. To construe them under the category of linguistic communication necessarily involves construing their production as speech acts (1971: 615).

In contrast, none of the devices used in non-interpersonal sorts of divination are communication tools. The geomancer's compass registers the north—south axis; handbooks of geomancy, horoscopy, or physiognomy organize factual information about the world; the characters written or chosen by a client in character-divination result from his personality or personal situation.

Another striking contrast between the two sorts of divination is that the one involves what an outsider would call a 'randomizing' device and the other does not. At some point each of the types of divination involving interpersonal trans- action (except possession, where the god uses a human voice to express himself) uses a device that cannot be controlled by the human participants: the fall of blocks or coins, the blind choice of numbered sticks, etc. We say this is a random- izing device; the participants say this is done so that neither *humans* nor any force can control the outcome, but the *gods* can.[8] Non-interpersonal sorts of divination use devices whose operation is closely determined by forces in the environment (the geomancer's compass), or by the personality of the client (character divination). In no case are free-falling devices or blind-choice tech- niques used so that another being can exert influence over the outcome.

I have noted several times that interpersonal divination can be described as a communicative code. We can now refine this description, and produce three more points of contrast between the two forms of divination: codes in inter- personal divination are restricted to a greater or lesser degree, involve consti- tutive rules, and require an elaborate system of interpretation. Let me take up these points in turn.

As I use it here, a 'restricted code' is a specialized means of communication that differs from ordinary language, in that the number of vocabulary items and the rules for their combination are relatively limited.[9] These limitations are appropriate because in interpersonal divination there is a relatively greater dis- tance between the communicating parties than is typical in ordinary social interactions. In ordinary social interactions, one communicates much of the time with beings who speak the same language, who are close to one (in distance as well as social position), and who are human. In contrast, in interpersonal divination, one is often attempting communication with beings who speak another language, who are physically or socially distant, and who are not human (in that they are spiritual or do not have human bodies). This greater distance between communicating parties seems to go along with use of restricted codes. I will first illustrate the distance between gods and men and how restricted codes can be used to overcome it.

In the Chinese case, high gods are distant, as we have seen, primarily because of their great power, rank, and wealth. Perhaps as a reflection of the differences between Mandarin, the language spoken by powerful officials, and whatever language is spoken locally, gods are sometimes said to speak a foreign tongue. The gods' own language can be heard just at the moment when they are translating or having their words translated into a human one, that is, at the beginning and end of a possession session with a human being. Jordan reports that after a shaman (*tang-ki*) begins to shake in a trance,

suddenly he breaks into loud, high-pitched, unintelligible 'gods' language'. He now stands over the table, and the bench is removed. Within a minute or two the gods' language has become a variety of Hokkien. It is distorted by the imposition of melodic lines that destroy the normal tones of words, and it is complicated by the introduction of odd expressions, interrupted by belches and vocative shrieks addressed to the 'little brethren', a term used by the Third Prince to address his followers. The god is now ready for questions. These are normally addressed to him by the head of the household, standing anxiously beside the family altar. After each answer has been given, the medium's flow of speech trails off and becomes a series of unintelligible mutterings, and the bystanders discuss the import of what has been revealed. Because of the distorted language, only people who have been through many séances with Tian-huah are able to interpret what he says, and they sometimes must ask for clarification (1972: 75−6).

In addition to being set apart from ordinary humans because they have great power, the gods are also set apart because they are spirits. They cannot be seen and they do not always possess the usual means of communicating: a voice or bodily gestures and postures.

Restricted codes used to overcome these gaps between gods and men can take several forms, some more restricted than others. In the most restricted sort of code I have introduced, the two parties to the communication can only transmit and receive a limited number of words. They can communicate in a limited way, the one posing a limited number of topics for the other's consideration, the other responding in a limited way. As we have seen, in Chinese *thiu-chiam* divination the petitioner chooses from a certain number of topics he can ask the gods to consider. In their reply, the gods are seemingly restricted to a vocabulary of numbers, as many as there are sticks. But as we have also seen, each of these sticks is correlated by prearrangement with a set text, a list of topics, and an indication of how the text applies to each topic. To see that the vocabulary the gods can transmit includes many words, one need only assume, as the participants do, that the gods know the contents of the paper slips. One set of slips from a temple near San-hsia has the thirteen possible topics printed on each slip: an affair in an outside place, business, pregnancy, luck, official matters, year end, moving, wealth, fate, lost goods, success, marriage, rainfall. For the most part, each of the 100 slips gives a different answer for the thirteen topics, yielding a maximum of 1,300 topic-and-answer pairs.

It is necessary for the petitioner to state a topic within the set list and to read the ensuing slip *only* with regard to that topic. This allows the god to give a response more-or-less tailored to the individual. Since it is unlikely that the particular configuration of replies on any one slip will apply to a single petitioner, he will have to solicit, and the god send, a number of separate replies on separate topics. The first slip, asked for with regard to marriage, might be number thirteen, reading 'unpropitious' for that topic. The second, asked for with regard to moving, might be number forty-five, reading 'good' for that topic and so on. There would thus be a great many possible configurations of answers using the 1,300 or so pairs.

It should be obvious that the list of possible topics for the god's consideration should logically include items of primary concern for the petitioners. If one can only use a limited number of words, one would obviously want them to reflect core concerns. Looking at a selection of topics on divination slips from Taiwan is like reading a kind of dictionary of key terms. *Chiam* slips for a *Co-su-kong* temple in Ting-p'u, Taiwan, include: carrying out affairs, sick person, searching for a person, pregnancy, journey, litigation, year end, moving residence, seeking wealth, sickness, lost goods, fame, marriage, seeking rain, an affair in an outside place, an official affair, fate, a person's arrival. The most frequently listed categories in a *Kuan-ti* temple in Tainan, Taiwan are honor, litigation, sickness, marriage, pregnancy, a travelling person, seeking wealth. Occasional entries include happiness, grave land, dreams, plans.[10]

To move on to another sort of code, we find communication can be somewhat less restricted. One party can transmit any message whatsoever and assume that it will be understood. The other party, however, can only return an extremely limited set of replies. In *puaq-pue*, for example, the human petitioner can ask any question he or she likes, but the god's reply is restricted to three 'words': yes, no, and laughing.

When the gods take on corporeal form, the distance between men and gods is reduced and the use of these sorts of restricted codes nearly disappears. In one sort of case the gods can understand any message put to them, but can only reply in an alien tongue. In Gray's description of spirit writing, the pencil makes 'mystic characters understood only by the professor and his assistant. These are translated into Chinese by the assistant who is always present, so that the votary may have a perfect knowledge of what the spirit has stated in reply to his questions and prayers' (1878: II, 21). In Elliott's description of spirit mediums in Singapore, 'Most *tang-ki* speak so that no one can understand them except their immediate colleagues. Often, they mutter petulantly and at great length in a shrill, artificial voice. This is supposed to be *"shen* language", an approximation to old Chinese' (1955: 64). As in the Gray example, of course, the *tang-ki*'s assistants can provide translations into the local colloquial Chinese.

In the least restricted form of communication relevant to the Chinese case, one party can receive and understand any message put to him and can respond in the language of his petitioners. There is no limit here to the words or sentences the gods can speak or write, except the natural language. Real conversations are possible. Perhaps because communication can still be problematic (the god's words may be garbled) a restricted code is sometimes resorted to: the god gives one strike of the sedan-chair pole for a correct guess of a written character and two for a wrong one.

Turning to non-interpersonal divination, I have made a case that geomancy and other such systems of knowledge do not involve messages and so cannot be codes. There is still the question, however, whether there might be a formal similarity between these systems and codes in interpersonal divination: in particular, the factors that figure in a calculation might be restricted to a limited number. Consider geomancy. A geomancer's compass, which is divided into concentric circles in turn divided into segments, would appear to be an excellent example of such a restricted number of factors. It is restricted in certain ways, to be sure, but not in the way the elements of codes in interpersonal divination are. First, it is clear that the geomancer must consider points in a continuum around the circles. *Ch'i* (vital breath) declines in a range to total inactivity (Feuchtwang 1974a: 142); the directional points are on a continuum such that due points mean certainty, while transitional points mean change (p. 30). Even if the geomancer does restrict himself to considering the features of a site enumerated on the rings of his compass (as we will see below, he need not), each ring involves a continuum of points that grade into each other, not discrete and separate units as in the restricted codes discussed above.

Nor is the geomancer limited in the number of readings he can take, as the petitioner is in *thiu-chiam* divination, for example. Feuchtwang lists numerous bearings that must be taken, on hills or mountains and their slopes, water courses, and many other features of the landscape (p. 31). The number of bearings is presumably limited only by what the geomancer regards as relevant and could, in theory, be infinite.

Finally the geomancer is not in practice limited to the factors itemized on the rings of his compass. A whole miscellany of other kinds of configurations can be seen in landscapes and are felt to have a bearing on the site: the form of written characters — indicating what they stand for in the language — or the shape of objects — a junk, teeth holding in saliva, a fish net holding in fortune, and so on (Ahern 1973: 36—9, 48, 56, 60—6; Aijmer 1968; Feuchtwang 1974a: 168—71; Giles 1878: 25). The possibilities here are genuinely unlimited: 'anything the environment suggests to you may become significant in the light of appropriate circumstances' (Feuchtwang 1974a: 171).

We do not have a sufficiently detailed study of horoscopic analysis *in use* to determine to what extent the expert is limited to set categories — the twelve cyclic animals, the five elements, the twelve segments of time in a day — and to what extent the edges of these categories blur into each other.[11] One can only speculate whether time or the sequence of elements is treated in practice as a continuum rather than as a set of closed segments. If one were born near the end of a period governed by fire, one's fate might be affected by earth, the next element in the series.

In one simple form of horoscopic divination described by Doré (and known in Taiwan) there does appear to be a restricted set of categories. If an object is lost, for example, one adds the numbers representing the month, day, and hour it was lost. One then counts on the two upper joints of the three middle fingers of the left hand until the total is exhausted. Each of these six joints is associated with a set prognostication and the joint on which the count ends marks the correct one (Doré 1965–7: IV, 377–8). Although there is an absolutely limited set of units here, they are, of course, not messages. These are calculations of invariant and perfectly predictable processes, such as calculations we might make about what date Easter will fall on in 1985. The set categories make this divination similar in form to *thiu-chiam*, but the content of the categories still set it off: instead of basic dictionaries of people's concerns and problems, horoscopic categories are determined by an abstract theory and in themselves bear no relevance to people's lives. The lack of a randomizing device also distinguishes it from *thiu-chiam*. This case demonstrates the existence of a range of types, from paradigms of communication at one end to calculation at the other, with numerous intermediate cases in the middle.

There is another apparent intermediate case between the end points I have been describing as interpersonal and non-interpersonal divination. It has been averred that the *I Ching*, perhaps the most influential form of Chinese divination, does not involve communication with spiritual agencies (Wilhelm and Baynes 1967: 315). Yet it clearly involves both 'random' devices and a limited code of sixty-four items, read in combination. Although this is not the place to go into a historical study of Chinese divination I must mention that some scholars see the *I Ching* as historically closely related to forms of divination that *were* communications with the gods and ancestors: the oracle-bone consultations of the Shang state (1523–1027 B.C.) (Keightley 1978: 2) and the milfoil-stalk divination of the Chou dynasty (1121–255 B.C.). Some have suggested that the *I Ching* was a method of communication with the gods in the Chou dynasty (Joseph Needham 1956: 350–1; C.K. Yang 1961: 107, 251). It is possible that its form was taken on when it was a means of communication with sentient beings, and that its form was maintained even though it lost its straightforward communicative function.

Let us turn to the next point of contrast between the two forms of divination: constitutive rules. 'Constitutive rules' are defined by John Searle, who distinguishes them from 'regulative rules' (1969: 33–42). Regulative rules regulate 'independently existing forms of behavior': that is, behavior that exists logically independently of the rules associated with it. For example, the rules of etiquette regulate interpersonal behavior, but interpersonal behavior remains just that no matter what rules, if any, are followed, or regarded as relevant. Constitutive rules, on the other hand, create or define new forms of behavior. For example, the rules of chess do not regulate playing chess: they create the very possibility of playing it. The activity is logically dependent on the rules.

A second dimension of the difference is that regulative rules can be paraphrased as imperatives: 'When eating, do this . . . '. They take the form 'Do X . . . ' or 'If X, do Y'. Constitutive rules on the other hand involve definitions: 'A checkmate is made when . . . '. They take the form 'X counts as Y'. Activities such as games may of course involve both sorts of rules, but there is nonetheless a core of rules that are constitutive, without which the activity could not exist. Another way of seeing this distinction is to realize that

Where the rule is purely regulative, behavior which is in accordance with the rule could be given the same description or specification (the same answer to the question 'What did he do?') whether or not the rule existed, provided the description or specification makes no explicit reference to the rule. But where the rule (or system of rules) is constitutive, behavior which is in accordance with the rule can receive specifications or descriptions which it could not receive if the rule or rules did not exist (Searle 1969: 35).

For example, one could say, 'He sent out the invitations two weeks before the the party', to describe someone's behavior whether or not a (regulative) rule of etiquette to that effect existed. But one could not say: 'They played football', unless the rules of football existed. Without 'an antecedently existing game of football, there is no sense in which their behavior could be described as playing football' (p. 36).

This is not to say that activities characterized by constitutive rules are governed by conventions, whereas activities characterized by regulative rules are not. Agriculture – an activity usually characterized by regulative rules – is often associated with a large number of conventions that govern its techniques, its personnel, its timing, and its purposes. Despite this there is an important difference between the way rules relate to agriculture and the way they relate to activities characterized by constitutive rules, such as games. That difference can be put this way: the procedures, personnel, place, and manner of planting corn may all be prescribed by convention, but even if one did not adhere to convention for some reason the activity would still count as planting corn. A man who flaunted tradition to use a different seed, try a new technique, or ignore a customary ritual might be called a fool and his attempt at farming might be termed a likely failure, but if his efforts succeeded, no one would deny that he had indeed raised a crop of corn. With games, however, the situation is quite otherwise. One can of course get a football from one end of the field to the other in countless different ways. But unless it is done according to the rules of the game it simply does not count as football. The rules constitute the game: unless they are heeded, the game has not been played.

In the foregoing examples of highly restricted codes, one or both parties must communicate within a limited vocabulary governed by constitutive rules. For example, in *thiu-chiam* and *puaq-pue* a consultation *consists in* a given set of procedures; the various falls of the blocks or the draws of the slips *count as* the god's various answers. It is as if, because of the distance between gods and man, the ordinary give and take of conversation is impossible. The parties have had to arrive by prearrangement at a shorthand code that serves for most needs. In a similar manner, wilderness campers learn that a single whistle-blast signals distress or that the thirteen figures in the ground–air emergency code signal such things as 'in need of food and water'. The assumption is that anyone searching for lost campers would recognize these signals because they are widely conventionally accepted. When, for one reason or another, the flexibility and adaptability of the natural language is not possible, and a few mutually understood terms must suffice, those terms will often be given their readings by definition (according to constitutive rules): if people can agree on the (approximate) meaning of a set of terms once and for all, then they can assume as much in subsequent communication. This has its advantage where communication is severely limited or truncated and it is not possible to renegotiate the basic meaning of terms.

The contrast to non-interpersonal divination is clear. Many of the rules for practicing geomancy are regulative, taking the form 'Do X . . . ' or 'If X, do Y' rather than the constitutive form 'X counts as Y': 'Avoid attracting *sha* (noxious wind) to a gravesite'; 'If a line in the configuration of a site points straight at the place of building or burial (thus being prone to transmit harmful *sha*), block it by an embankment, a screen wall, trees, or a board with an appropriate charm' (Feuchtwang 1974a: 115). Even though rules for the interpretation of landscape configurations appear to take the form 'X counts as Y' — 'Parallel streams with no mountains between and flowing out of the site mean the sale of father's land, the plundering of wealth, and disgrace' (Feuchtwang 1974a: 132) — they are actually causal statements: parallel streams under certain conditions will cause certain consequences.

Beyond this, it seems probable that if a geomancer were to strike out on a new tack, suggesting an unconventional causal connection, his results would be judged as successes or failures in bringing benefits, much as a new agricultural technique would be, not as nonsensical. Compare the reaction if someone performing *puaq-pue* decided in the context of a consultation to count a fall of one flat side up, one down as a yes response. Bystanders would react much as if a ship's captain decided on his own to regard three dots, three dashes, three dots as a signal for 'all's well'.

Finally, I turn to the matter of elaborate interpretation. If one received a message in a restricted code such as the ground—air emergency code, considerable effort would have to go into interpreting it. One message reads only 'in need of food and water'. But this message may not reflect the sender's situation exactly; it would only be the closest approximation to it from all the possible messages in the code. It would be up to the recipient to make a further interpretation. For example, if the message were sent from terrain in which there were known to be numerable potable streams, a reasonable interpretation would be that the sender needed only food.

Similarly, it is necessary to interpret messages received from a restricted divinatory code. We have seen that the gods and ancestors are regarded as persons and act on the basis of human-like motives and intentions. So when 'yes, no, laughing' replies are received through *puaq-pue*, reasons and motives for them are suggested: the god refuses to possess this *tang-ki* because he prefers to possess someone else; the ancestor is amused because she is eating in a new place; the god chose this man as *lo-cu* (master of the incense pot) because he is upright and virtuous.

When more complex messages are sent, as in *thiu-chiam*, interpretation is even more difficult. Receiving one out of the 100 or so possible answers related to marriage gives one only a rough indication of how the god would respond if he could speak more fully. It is rather like a code that guides one from the names of streets to the location of streets on a map. Since one is only given a location within a square on the map, one has to search for any particular street within that square. The domain is only roughly bounded. Handbooks used by temple-keepers or priests to aid in the interpretation of *chiam* consist of more and more elaborate layers of interpretation. A handbook for a *Kuan-ti* temple in Taiwan lists, *chiam* by *chiam*, the literary text itself, a breakdown by topic with brief responses, a paragraph elaborating on the general meaning of the text, a paragraph translating the literal meaning of the text, and two further commentaries (*Kuan-sheng-ti-chün* 1971). The interpretative paragraph for a *chiam* listed as very good is as follows:

This oracle means that affairs one is planning or hoping for will be fulfilled. But there are particulars for each. If a government worker casts this one, he will have excessive happiness. A scholar will have the blessing of honors. He who is casting with regard to the future [road] will have happiness and long life. He who is divining about his affairs will find them absolutely stable. As for those who are planning to seek wealth, they should regard it as important that that which is famous is not substantial; talk is empty (*Kuan-sheng-ti-chün* 1971: part 2, p. 1).

The interpretation for a *chiam* listed as very bad is as follows:

According to this *chiam*, as soon as propitious affairs have ended, terrible calamities will come. Official matters are approaching, such that you will not be able to avoid their arrival. Whatever you are planning or hoping for will not succeed. Financial negotiations will not come off. Whatever you do will have no profit. In a case of urgency, it is fitting to pray to the gods. Store up virtue and return to [the way of] heaven. Only thus will you avoid regret (*ibid.*).

In practice *chiam* (Mandarin *ch'ien*) are interpreted so as to fit the particular situation of the person consulting the god. Temple-keepers, if consulted, try to give the *chiam* relevance to the client. Kleinman gives some examples:

Clients (Several relatives have come to ask about the fate of health of another family member. They look concerned.)

Ch'ien interpreter (looking at the *ch'ien*): 'It is not good. What do you specifically want to ask about?'

Clients: 'This relative is a man with liver disease. Our family would like to send him to Japan to cure this liver disease. We wish to ask if it is good to send him to Japan?'

Ch'ien interpreter: 'It's fine to send him to Japan. To change doctors if the patient is not improving is good for the patient.' (This interpretation actually runs counter to the *ch'ien* which should have been interpreted as *no* in this case. The *ch'ien* interpreter, however, obtained the same impression my research assistant obtained that the family members were looking for a positive answer to sanction their desire to send this family member to Japan.)

Client (a middle aged female asking about her daughter's fate for marrying . . .)

Ch'ien interpreter: 'Does your daughter have a boy friend yet?'

Client: 'Yes. A friend introduced this man to her.'

Ch'ien interpreter: 'Does your daughter agree with him or not? If she agrees, then you come back to ask again.'

Client: 'My daughter won't say anything. She has no opinion about it.'

Ch'ien interpreter: 'You can make a decision only after your daughter has agreed. This *ch'ien* says . . . "not suitable", maybe that's the reason why your daughter does not give her opinion. You can tell her that the god here said "not right yet". What's your opinion?'

(The client did not answer but went off smiling as if she appreciated this interpretation.)

Ch'ien interpreter: 'What is the problem?'

Client (a lower middle-class woman about 35 years of age): 'Marriage. The man has a concubine.'

Ch'ien interpreter: 'Don't marry him. The *ch'ien* says not to marry.'

Client: 'I am already married to him. Should I separate?'

Ch'ien interpreter: 'Do you have children?'

Client: 'Yes'.

Ch'ien interpreter: 'Does he give you money?'

Client: 'Yes, he gives me at least half the money.'

Ch'ien interpreter: 'Then don't separate from him. It is not good to separate.'

(This culturally conservative advice appears to be the opposite of what is written on the *ch'ien*, but seemed to make sense in this case. And after the client left, people standing around the interpreter as well as my research assistants approved his remarks.) (Kleinman 1978: 349–51.)

The assumption is that the god knows everything about the client's affairs and so is in a position to give good advice. The interpreter's job is to construe the *chiam* so that it fits the client's case and, above all, to give reasonable advice. The god is a person of sagacity, after all, and the interpreter is only acting in his stead. The condensed *chiam* message must be expanded to be what the god would say if he were conversing freely. .

The question of 'contradiction' between the *chiam* and the advice given need never arise. In the third example above, it appears that the *chiam* says one thing and the interpreter the opposite. Actually, the *chiam* probably read '*bou-hap*' or 'not harmonious'. This could mean, 'The marriage *has not been* harmonious', just as well as, 'The marriage *will not be* harmonious'. Once the interpreter knows the client is already married, he construes the *chiam* as a comment on that marriage: his advice is not inconsistent with the *chiam* in the least.

Sometimes the god himself (when possessing a man and speaking through him) literally carries on a conversation, largely obviating the need for elaborate interpretation. In one session I attended in Ch'inan, the god *Ong-ia-kong* was asked about the illness of a little girl. He announced that three years ago she had fallen into a water ditch and bumped into a 'death' ghost which had been following her around ever since. *Ong-ia-kong* asked whether the child had had a serious illness three years ago. The mother answered yes. He asked whether the family had been quarreling a lot lately. The mother agreed. *Ong-ia-kong* explained, 'This is because of the presence of ghosts around the house. In order to get rid of them, prepare this medicine for the child: offer rice and vegetables as well as paper money to the ghost plaguing her; hang one charm on the bedroom door, burn one outside the house, and keep one on the child's body.'

On the matter of elaborate interpretation, there is very little difference in form to be seen between interpersonal and non-interpersonal divination. The interpreter and the client convert messages from a god into advice on the basis of their knowledge of the particulars of the case; geomancers or fortune-tellers also convert information from geomantic or horoscopic calculations into advice on the basis of similar considerations.

In sum, the following features are characteristic of Chinese interpersonal divination:

(1) There is some communication device whose operation is meant to be removed from any control but the gods'.

(2) Unless the spirit is embodied and vocal or able to write, there is a restricted code composed of a limited set of vocabulary items whose meaning is conventionally agreed upon by prearrangement. The rules for obtaining replies are constitutive; the vocabulary reflects matters of 'core' concern.

(3) Messages received through the code receive elaborate interpretation so that they become the kind of full-scale messages it is assumed the god could make.

A further — and crucial — difference between interpersonal and non-interpersonal divination emerges out of a consideration of the relationship among systems of knowledge about the world, experts who have mastered and can apply these, and ordinary people who have need of this knowledge. The simplest relationship is between human clients and human experts in some body of knowledge. Men and women consult geomancers, horoscopists, medical doctors, etc. with particular problems. The expert, on the basis of his knowledge about processes or forces in the world, determines how those forces bear on the client and then gives advice. For example, a geomancer might say, 'the *ch'i* is dispersed from your ancestors' grave site and so no benefits are flowing to you [a bit of factual information]. You should move the grave [advice based on factual information].'

A more complex relationship exists between clients, gods, and systems of knowledge. It is clear that gods utilize the *same* bodies of knowledge as do human men and women of learning, though their learning may be superior. The god *Co-su-kong* is a herbal doctor and prescribes herbs of the same sort as do human doctors. One man told me all mankind's medical knowledge originally came from the gods. Again, if a grave has poor geomancy, one can ask a god for help. In accord with the same principles used by men, he will make a change in the surrounding topography and 'fix' the geomancy. Yet again, gods can give horoscopic information about an individual or a proposed match: one can get their advice through *chiam*, *pauq-pue*, a possessed *tang-ki*, or, as Freedman says, by putting the relevant information on the house altar and waiting three days to see if anything untoward happens (1957: 129–30).

To get access to the gods' knowledge, one must use a form of interpersonal divination: this distinguishes it most radically from non-interpersonal forms of divination such as geomancy. Interpersonal divination used when the god is at a distance (not embodied in a *tang-ki* or a device) is at *one more remove* from a system of knowledge than is the direct consultation of an expert. For this reason interpersonal forms of divination such as *puaq-pue* and *thiu-chiam* cannot be included in a list together with non-interpersonal divination procedures as if they were all of the same order. Geomancy and horoscopy are themselves systems of knowledge. *Puaq-pue* and *thiu-chiam* are systems of access to the gods' knowledge.[12]

5

Open and closed practices

Searle's distinction between constitutive and regulative rules has been used by Tom Morawetz as the basis of a distinction between 'open' and 'closed' practices (1973: 860–1).[1] In this chapter we will see how Morawetz's distinction can be used to illuminate certain aspects of change in Chinese ritual; in the next chapter we will see how open and closed rituals relate differently to the Chinese state.

Examples of closed practices are games like chess and baseball. A closed practice is one in which each instantiation (each game, for example) has an explicit beginning and end. Participants qualify as participants when they are familiar with all the rules of the practice which define moves, positions, goals, etc., rules which can be given more or less exhaustively and are *constitutive* of the practice. During a game, these rules are fixed (Morawetz 1973: 860).

Examples of open practices are particular legal systems and particular languages. In open practices,

participation is ordinarily open-ended and the rules of the practice are standing rules which govern on-going activity. Participants are not required to know the particular rules which define permissible moves and positions in order for them to qualify as participants, and in fact they may not do so. Moreover, it may be impossible in principle to give an exhaustive and complete account of the rules of the practice, either because they are unlimited in number or, more importantly, because the set of rules is constantly evolving. The practice may provide institutional ways in which rules can be changed (pp. 860–1).

The points of difference between the two types can be set out systematically as follows:

Closed practices	*Open practices*
1. Each instantiation has an explicit beginning and end.	1. The activity is on-going and open-ended.
2. People must know all the rules of the practice to take part.	2. Even though people may not know the rules, they can still participate.
3. The rules involved can be described exhaustively.	3. It would be impossible to give a complete account of the rules involved.

4. The rules are constitutive.	4. The rules are regulative.
5. The rules are fixed during instances of the practice.	5. The rules can change during instances of the practice.
6. The point of the practice is given in the rules.	6. The point of the practice may lie outside the rules.

Considering each point in turn we can see how some games, divination procedures, and parliamentary procedures fall into the pattern of closed practices and how some portions of etiquette, law, and language fall into the pattern of open practices.

(1) The rules of games and other closed practices specify how the activity starts and what counts as a beginning. A game of chess begins when the players choose sides of the board; a meeting begins when a quorum is present and the chairperson calls the meeting to order. An observer who knew the system would have no trouble identifying the start and finish of these activities. In contrast, many rules of etiquette, law, or language apply in an on-going way to open-ended activities. Most principles of etiquette do not apply only to clearly demarcated kinds of behavior; they apply to human interactions of all sorts.

(2) A player must know all the rules of chess in order to play; one could say he must be able to recite them. In contrast, speakers of languages often do not know the rules that underlie their speech and a citizen can move through legal proceedings without being aware of all the laws that apply to his case.

(3) A complete list of all rules that define games and parliamentary procedure can be, and often is, drawn up. In contrast, the rules involved in languages are not so easily limited (some would argue they are infinite in number); the rules involved in law are undergoing constant change through interpretation as law is administered in courts. This distinction has the same flavor as Waismann's distinction between a description of a mathematical concept on the one hand and an empirical object on the other (1965b: 127–8). For a concept such as a triangle in Euclidean geometry, giving the lengths of the three sides provides a complete and exhaustive description; nothing relevant is left out. A description of an empirical object such as my right hand, however, could never be complete. An infinite number of facts, including its size, shape, weight, and placement in space, would be relevant.

Similarly Waismann points out that complete definitions are not always possible. A complete definition of a term provides 'an exhaustive list of all the circumstances in which the term is to be used so that nothing is left to doubt' (1965a: 128). A move in a game such as check-mate in chess can be so defined. But definitions of other things 'stretch into an open horizon' because they cannot anticipate all possible uses. Words, for example, are extended in use as when 'laundering' is applied to dirty clothes and then to dirty money. And our laws can seldom specify how they should be applied in all cases. The law may state that 'no vehicles are allowed in the park' but not specify whether a toy motor car or a pogo stick is to be counted as a vehicle (Hart 1961: 123; Morawetz 1973: 862).

(4) As I argued in Chapter 4, a core of constitutive rules defines activities like games whereas regulative rules apply in activities like etiquette (Searle 1969: 33–4).

(5) Here one must distinguish between instances of closed practices (*a* game of football) and the practice as an institution (*the* game of football). Officials on the proper governing boards can change the rules of the game over time, but players in any specific game cannot change the rules. This of course is more true for games played in a professional league, where conditions of play should be comparable, than for casual neighborhood games. For such casual games, as well as for games such as hopscotch that have no institutionalized governing board, one can only say that once a group of players have agreed on a set of rules, an individual player – a willful child aside – cannot insist that a different set applies to him.

In contrast, the practice of etiquette can display constant, on-going change as, during interactions, new ways of verbally or gesturally greeting or parting may be adopted.

(6) In a closed practice, the *point* of the practice is given in the rules (Morawetz 1973: 864–6). If one is asked to justify a move in a closed practice one can do so by referring to the rules: 'I moved my rook on the board this way because this is how you checkmate'; 'I bowed forward this way because this is how you *pai-pai*.' One can do the same with open practices: 'I stopped at the traffic-light because the law says I must'; 'I don't shout on the tennis court because that is proper etiquette in tennis.' The difference is that one can justify *not* adhering to the usual rules in an open practice by citing a point the practice has that lies outside the rules: 'I went through the traffic-light because I was trying to get a critically ill person to the hospital quickly. The point of traffic laws is to preserve lives; had I obeyed, the point would not have been served'; 'We shouted on the tennis court because no one else was playing. The point of rules of etiquette is to avoid distracting others but since no one else was nearby our shouting didn't matter.' One could not do this in a closed practice: imagine a baseball player asking for four strikes and justifying his request by saying the point of baseball is to beat the other team so he needed an extra swing to do that.

In general, systems of etiquette provide good examples of this aspect of open practices. Consider Chinese politeness (*kheq-khi*), for example. One could say that the point of most *kheq-khi* talk and behavior is to gain the favor of or express respect to others. Even though one common rule of polite behavior is to present a gift of money in a red envelope (an *ang-pau*) to someone of higher social status from whom one wishes a favor, the rule could frequently be reinterpreted when it would not serve the point of being polite. For example, one would probably not offer a European or American doctor an *ang-pau* (above and beyond his fee) because he might take offense, rather than be more willing to help.

It is important to say that these sets of related characteristics may apply to a whole practice in some cases and to part of a practice in others. It is probably most accurate to speak of a range of types with extremes on either end and mixed cases in the middle: it might in some cases be useful to describe a practice as having a closed core and an open periphery.[2]

In what way is this distinction of use in our discussion of Chinese ritual? First let us look at examples representing points along the range from closed to open practices. Methods of divination frequently yield examples of closed practices. As we have seen, in divination, the gods signal a yes or no reply by determining the fall of two blocks. The rules for interpreting the fall of the blocks are constitutive: generally two flat sides down count as a no; two flat sides up count as laughing; one up, one down count as a yes. These rules are definitional and are fixed during instances of the practice; just as a batter could not choose to be allowed four strikes, so a woman throwing divining blocks could not choose to interpret flat sides down as a positive response. In some cases further rules for their use are set by temples: at a *Tho-te-kong* temple in *San-hsia*, the convention is that if the first three throws fall one block up and one down it counts as a yes; at the *Kuan-ti* temple if one throw out of the first three is one up one down, it counts as a yes. Just as football players must be informed of the relevant conventions in different areas before play begins, so petitioners at unfamiliar temples must ask whether special *puaq-pue* procedures are in effect.

The practice of *puaq-pue* is thus closed by the criteria in points (4) and (5) above. As in (1) it has a clear beginning and end, the beginning marked by holding the *pue* up to eye level toward the god's image, the end marked by grasping the two *pue* together in both hands and moving the hands up and down toward the image. As in (2) participants must know the rules to take part; as in (3) the rules can be described exhaustively and as in (6) the point of the practice is given in the rules. (You throw the *pue* this way because this is how you communicate with the god.)

When we turn to other kinds of ritual, we find that most appear to have some constitutive and some regulative rules, and thus, one could say, some parts that are more closed than others. For example, the act called *pai-pai* is in part a closed practice. In order to perform it, and thus communicate with the god or other spirit being addressed, one must press both hands together in front of one's chest, elbows to one's sides, and, facing the image or its incense pot, bow slightly from the waist and move the hands up and down. This is the signal the two distant parties — spirits and men — recognize as necessary to start a communication. Elaborations are possible and frequently added: a speech, silently or audibly made to the god; incense held between the hands and placed in the god's incense pot; food placed before the image; a kneeling posture. But these optional elements vary widely depending on the worshipper's mood and resources, or on the kind of social occasion involved. The only constitutive rule has to do with the body position and movement adopted: to *pai-pai* is by definition to hold the hands together and move them up and down while bowing in relation to a god's image or incense pot. This is like saying that a single loud sound counts as a distress call in the wilderness: whether one shouts, blows a whistle, or sounds a horn is an entirely optional matter. I never saw anyone address the gods without the body posture and hand position I have described but when I pressed informants I was told that the absolute minimum for an act to count as '*pai-pai*' was a slight bow of the head. This may be the most constitutive element in the act, an element that also plays a key role in showing respect in ordinary life.

I asked whether an act still counts as '*pai-pai*' even though everything but the posture and gesture varies. My informants replied that contact with the gods (and thus the act of *pai-pai*) can only be accomplished as long as the hands and body are held and moved in the proper way. The worshipper need do nothing else. Even the person's inner dispositions are irrelevant. My occasional act of addressing the gods was considered '*pai-pai*' (and I was carefully coached to hold and move my hands and body in the correct way) even though it was generally known that I did not 'believe' in gods.

Some rules related to *pai-pai* are constitutive, but others are regulative rules with open texture. For example, there are general expectations for which kinds of food and ritual money are offered to various gods or spirits. But this is a matter very much open to interpretation and change. A spirit who at one time is offered ritual food and money appropriate to a ghost may later come to be offered food and money suited to a new higher status of an efficacious god.

In this respect, the rules of food offerings are much like the regulative rules of etiquette. As I have described them in Chapter 3, most rules of Chinese etiquette take a regulative form: 'if X, do Y'. For example, if one wants to flatter gods or men, one should use a polite form of address, manner of speech, and bodily posture; if one wants to play a proper host role, one should defer to one's guests, 'receive' them at a distance from one's house, and 'send them off' when they leave. Here interpersonal relations are being governed by rules, but interpersonal relations do not consist in those rules. They exist logically independently of them.

This is not to argue that there are no constitutive elements in systems of etiquette. Some actions that form a part of a system of etiquette are defined constitutively. These often take the form of conventionally prearranged codes, which, as we will see, are similar to those in divination. For example, the accepting or declining of invitations is governed by such a code. In a case cited by Doolittle, a mandarin sent a written invitation and a gift of ten or fifteen dollars to a man, inviting him to sign on as his personal secretary.

If the man receives the present and the document, and retains them, it is understood that he accepts the terms and consents to fill the station. He considers himself engaged for a year. But if he declines to receive the present with the red paper and card, sending them back, the meaning is that he is dissatisfied with something, or that it is impossible for him to accept, being engaged or in feeble health (1966: I, 325).

Similarly, in the case of dinner invitations, one accepts by keeping the invitation card and declines by sending it back (Walshe n.d.: 91–2). Both accepting and declining can be done with greater or lesser degrees of politeness: in the Ch'ing one could give a verbal acceptance to the messenger or, to be more polite, write on a card that the invitation was 'thankfully accepted' (Walshe n.d.: 92). Here one can see clearly the coexistence of the two sorts of rules: accepting the invitation consists by definition in retaining the invitation card (constitutive); to accept politely, one should return a written reply (regulative).

Perhaps a more thoroughly open practice is represented by a kind of non-interpersonal divination already discussed: geomancy. Here rules are regulative (point 4): 'to capture the benefits, place the grave in a spot where the breaths concentrate'. To the extent that the rules are open to introduction of new factors (5), they could not be exhaustively written (3). It could easily be argued that the practice is on-going; casual observers of any natural scene are likely to comment in passing on its geomantic properties (1). I would also maintain that participants need not know all the rules to participate (2). Clients consult a geomancer as the greater expert, much as we consult a lawyer; but even practicing geomancers, just like lawyers, may have mastered only a portion of the system of rules.

We have discussed how change occurs in a closed practice, like a game, when a governing board uses its authority to institutionalize innovations. How does change occur in a closed portion of a ritual like Taiwanese *pai-pai*? There is no exact equivalent to a governing board for ritual, but there are ways conventions can be altered. When a new temple is established, the new managers can decide, in consultation with the god, that a certain code for communication using *pue* will be adopted in that temple. Somewhat differently, an individual can be favored by a special communication from a god and emboldened to establish a new convention for communication with this god on the spot. The case material I introduce below illustrates the process by which a god's revelations can legitimize new conventions. It also shows something about the particular pattern of change: why should people adopt changes in one portion of a ritual rather than another? The pattern seems to be that when a group of people wish to demonstrate that they are making a radical departure from tradition, they do so by changing a *closed* portion of a practice.

I begin with an unusual sect in San-hsia. A group of devotees call themselves the *Kiu-tou Hue* (Seek the Way Association), claiming that their way of *pai-pai*-ing is the 'one true way of *pai-pai*-ing the gods', and that all other ways of *pai-pai*-ing and all other religions are superseded by their practices. These statements set adherents of this sect distinctly apart from ordinary people in the area who may well visit numerous different temples, but are concerned only about the relative powers of the various gods, not about finding some special way of paying respect to them.

The extraordinary nature of this sect is indicated by the attitudes non-members express toward it. Those who have witnessed the ceremonies describe them as strange and weird, and say that they personally felt very uncomfortable being there. One young woman who participates regularly and seriously lives with her grandmother. The grandmother objects strenuously to the girl's involvement (even though she credits the sect with having obtained a cure for her own illness) saying that the girl will have trouble getting married if she participates. 'Other people will think she's strange and that her way of thinking is not like theirs.' Another woman said: 'There is something strange and fearful about the people who go there and the place itself. There is something queer about the whole business.' Yet another young woman said she found the way they *pai-pai*-ed both remarkable and distressing. She reacted very strongly against one part of their ceremonies in which 'they knelt down and hit their heads on the floor many, many times. It felt very strange to look at them; I didn't like it and only wanted to leave.' While she was explaining her feelings to me, she intermittently demonstrated 'the usual way we *pai-pai*' holding her hands together and bowing her head slightly. In contrast, even though people often go to temples they have never visited before, some in the far southern end of the island, there is every indication they feel very much at ease in them, using the same form of posture as at home.

My assistant, who willingly accompanied me to funeral ceremonies and seances in the dead of night, refused to go to the sect after her fourth visit. She said that each time she went the people recognized her and pressed her to take part. If she went one more time without participating she was sure they would know she was not serious and would take offense. The term '*hue*' itself (association or organization) indicates the existence of a group with definite and exclusive criteria of membership, something not found among either casual or regular petitioners at an ordinary temple. Permission to join (*zip-tou*, enter the way) is sought from the gods, by throwing *pue*. If a 'yes' is received, the neophyte begins to study the teachings of the sect. Fellow adherents are addressed as *tou-iu* (friends of the way) because they too are striving to work their way up through the five levels of the *tou*, by learning how to perform good deeds. The ultimate goal is to *kiu-tou* (receive the way), at which point the soul attains direct and permanent admittance to heaven; there is no further rebirth. This otherworldly goal is itself far removed from the usual concerns of ordinary people, who simply hope the gods will help them with the worries of everyday life.

Perhaps as a way of signalling the radically different nature of their beliefs, members of the *Kiu-tou Hue* have altered the usual gesture and posture of *pai-pai*, those elements that we have seen form its constitutive core. It is their 'special method of paying respect' called *pai-le* (rites of respect) or more specifically *tieng-sieng pai* (upper level respect) that the devotees explain is 'reserved exclusively for members' and that is an essential part of attaining the *tou*. This method was revealed to the sect founder in 1974. The details of the method are secret, but what one can observe reveals striking differences from ordinary *pai-pai*. The devotees lay their two hands flat one on top of the other and hold incense between their fingers; they thrust their elbows out, away from the sides of their bodies, raising their hands high over their heads. When they wish to place incense in the pot, they move the bottom hand to the top position, place the incense, and then return that hand to the bottom position. The devotees then move back one step, bow and repeat this three times. Finally, they kneel and bow low with hands extended; covering one hand with the other, they pat the floor numerous times. (One member told me 180 pats were required.) Some of the ordinary elements of *pai-pai* are there — raising the hands while holding incense, bowing — but alterations in the usual hand position are made and additional movements not ordinarily performed are added: placing one hand flat on the other; patting the floor. Moreover, these movements are standardized for all members. I was told that a new member would observe and imitate the others, gradually learning further intricacies of the *pai-le*. Altering the constitutive element of ordinary *pai-pai* appears to be a means used by this sect to set themselves off from those who pay respect to the gods in the usual way.

If we turn to mainland China in Ch'ing times, we find a similar pattern. Certain postures and movements seem to have been defining characteristics of respecting the gods there, as in Taiwan. The illustrations of people interacting with gods in Doolittle's volumes show the same posture and hand movement used in Taiwan (1966: I, 126, II, 67, 84, 104). A similar hand movement is emphasized when a child is taught to *pai* — the term Doolittle says describes 'worship' (1872: I, 543) — the child is *'made to worship in a certain manner by moving its hands up and down a few times . . .* Sometimes, however, instead of its hands being moved up and down, the child, held in the hands of some one, is itself moved up and down before the object worshipped, which is reckoned the same as making it move its hands in worship' (1966: I, 126).

Also, as in Taiwan, those mainland religious sects that deliberately altered defining features of respecting the gods advocated more radical departures from tradition than those that did not. For example, the Triads were a loosely related group of political and religious organizations, especially active in the nineteenth century, dedicated to the overthrow of the Ch'ing (Manchu) dynasty and restoration of the last ethnically Chinese dynasty, the Ming (Chesneaux 1971: 15, 17; Wakeman 1972: 35). 'Anti-Manchu propaganda became one of the most important aspects of its activity', as illustrated in ritual texts:

> We will give the Manchus no rest:
> In the Hung-hua Pavilion
> We swore in Heaven's name
> To overthrow the Ch'ing and restore the Ming
> (Novikov 1972: 51, 53).

When initiands were first admitted into the society, they were asked, 'Why are

71

you here?' They were required to reply, 'To overthrow the Ch'ing and restore the Ming' (Novikov 1972: 54).

In accord with this restorationist orientation, the society stressed adherence to true Chinese customs. Initiates must 'imitate the rites practiced since antiquity by the Han' (Novikov 1972: 51). There was one unusual initiation ceremony in which initiands offered five blades of grass to the gods before offering incense, in imitation of an act performed by the founders (Schlegel 1866: 122; Ward and Stirling 1925: 59–60). But there was no mention of a special posture, or other special features of worship despite the existence of detailed transcripts of their rituals (Schlegel 1866). Rather than rejecting a fundamentally Chinese tradition, the Triads were advocating a return to genuinely Chinese traditions. They were concerned about evicting usurpers rather than gaining allegiance to new modes of thought and action.

In contrast to the restorationist tone of the Triads, the White Lotus sects largely broke with Chinese traditions. They worshipped only the 'Eternal Mother', rejecting all traditional gods. They predicted an apocalypse after which all believers would be saved and all others would be destroyed. Existing society was to be eliminated and replaced by a new order. 'Followers . . . anticipated a period of great cataclysms when they would cast aside their ordinary lives and, following the deity sent to lead them, join together and rise up to usher in a new and perfect world in which all people found salvation through their faith and their faith alone' (Naquin 1976: 2).

Their ritual reflected this radical departure from tradition. Whereas an ordinary person might regard a bow with hand gesture as the minimal element in interacting with the gods, the White Lotus adherents regarded recitation of an eight-character mantra as the minimal act. This mantra was a central aspect of membership: initiation ceremonies might consist of little more than the teaching of it to initiands (Naquin 1976: 33). Perhaps realizing its importance, the Ch'ing government made knowledge of the eight-character chant a criterion for meting out punishment for membership.

More elaborate rituals were equally removed from ordinary worship. The mantra might be repeatedly recited while 'the believer sat cross-legged like a monk, with eyes closed and arms clasped to the chest' (p. 26). Recitation of the mantra could also be a part of meditative exercises meant to control the vital breath (*ch'i*). If trance resulted from mediation, it meant one's soul was going to Heaven to pay respects to the Eternal Mother (p. 27).

Another sect, the Way of Fundamental Unity (*I-kuan Tao*) resembles White Lotus sects and may be historically related to them. Its members claimed to possess the one true way to salvation, promising terrible sufferings in hell to those who failed to follow the way. Rather than striving for a return to the true Chinese past, they preached 'the imminence of the end of the world and an apocalypse' (Chesneaux 1971: 53). Its leaders supported the Japanese during the second world war, claiming, in accord with Japanese propaganda, that Chinese and Japanese belonged to one race, and that Chinese should cooperate as the Japanese returned to occupy China, their original country (Deliusin 1972: 231). This sect, unlike the Triads and like the White Lotus, seems to have set itself against all existing and previous earthly orders, and looked ahead to the establishment of an entirely new order.

It should not be surprising, then, to find that, like the *Kiu-tou Hue* and White Lotus sects, the Way of Fundamental Unity altered the basic act of making contact with the gods. In a text summarized by Grootaers, the sect's founder details the mechanics of daily worship, which were revealed to him by the gods (1946: 334–9). When burning incense, the text reads: 'Il faut d'abord se laver les mains, et le visage, puis s'agenouiller avec le coeur recueilli. On élève l'encens des deux mains à hauteur des yeux, puis on l'allume de la main gauche' (p. 335).

A description by Li Shih-yü adds that the left hand is used because it is the god's: it neither holds a knife nor kills men (1948: 77). Beyond this feature, which was not present in ordinary acts of addressing the gods, incense was placed in the pot in specified patterns in a specified order depending on the rank of the god being honored (p. 77). This was not a part of ordinary acts of honoring the gods either. The radical character of their ideology makes it appropriate for them to have altered or at least elaborated upon the part of the ordinary act of worship that, I have argued, was its defining feature.

The Taiping movement, a rebel force that successfully established control over the lower basin of the middle Yangtse in the mid 1800s, had complicated antecedents in the secret societies (Curwen 1972). Among other things, it shared with the Way of Fundamental Unity a desire to establish a new social order rather than return to the genuine Chinese order of the Ming (Chesneaux 1971: 94). In words attributed to the founder of the movement, 'We may still speak of subverting the Tsing [Ch'ing], but we cannot properly speak of restoring the Ming. At all events, when our native mountains and rivers are recovered, a new dynasty must be established' (Curwen 1972: 68). The Taipings adopted the creating, omniscient, omnipotent god of Christianity and ranked Jesus and two of their founders below him (Shih 1967: 3). They destroyed images of Chinese gods wherever they went (Jen 1973: 37). They attacked geomancy and divination, opposed ancestor worship, and wrote a new calendar in which every day of the year was auspicious (Hamberg 1935: 36–9; Medhurst 1853: 43; Shih 1967: 24–7). They recommended and implemented new kinds of social and property relations among the living (Chesneaux 1971: 90; Feuerwerker 1975). Given the extensive nature of their break with existing traditions and their desire to lay down a social order along new lines it is scarcely surprising that the act of worship itself was altered.[3] Offering of incense was soon done away with:

At the commencement, Siu tsheun [the founder] had only vague notions concerning the true manner of religious service. When he had taken away his own idols, he placed the written name of God in their stead, and even used incense-

73

sticks and gold paper as part of the service. But in a few months he found that this was wrong, and abolished it (Hamberg 1935: 36).

Several observers' descriptions seem to indicate that kneeling was an important feature in the posture of prayer, a feature that was optional in traditional *pai-pai*.

When they engaged in prayer, they used to kneel down all in one direction towards the open side of the house from which the light entered, and closing their eyes, one spoke the prayer in the name of the whole assembly (Hamberg 1935: 36).

We understand our friend [Dr Taylor] was present at their worship, which he describes as consisting of changing hymns and doxologies in very solemn manner, whilst those engaged in it remained seated. After which all kneeled apparently with much reverence, closing their eyes, while one of their number uttered an audible prayer (Medhurst 1853).

After [reading a creed similar to the Apostles' Creed], the whole congregation kneeling, the minister reads a form of prayer, which is repeated after him by those present. When this litany is concluded, the people resume their seats and the minister reads them a sermon, after which the paper containing it is burnt (Lindley 1866: 320).

The particular form of the Taipings' innovations can, of course, be put down in part simply to Christian influence. But the Taipings certainly did not adopt Christianity without omissions or alterations: set alongside the cases discussed above, the Taiping case seems to give us another correlation between alteration in the constitutive element of worship and a radical departure from tradition.

If this correlation should hold up under further research, and others of a similar nature come to light, we would have the beginning of a way of understanding the significance of change in constitutive portions of Chinese rituals. If change is significant, lack of change is equally so: at the end of Part III we will see that lack of change in the specifically political aspects of tradition often means lack of change in the form of ritual directed to gods.

PART III

Politics

6

Ritual and political authorities

Recently, a number of people interested in the relationship between religion and politics have arrived at the same conclusion: that religion and ritual help those in power exercise authority over others. Maurice Bloch makes the stimulating suggestion that restricted codes of the sort discussed in Chapter 4 are apt tools in the hands of political leaders because they severely limit and predictably control the responses of political subordinates. He suggests further that it is common for those codes to occur in religious ritual because religion embodies traditional authority. Similarly, Rappaport suggests that 'sacred' rituals (those that refer to entities whose existence cannot be verified or falsified), make arbitrary control mechanisms seem necessary. Their arbitrariness is hidden in a 'cloak of seeming necessity' (1971: 35–6). This encourages authorities to use the sacred as a tool to achieve compliance (p. 41). Thus both Bloch and Rappaport suggest that leaders can use ritual to increase their legitimacy.

A related and complementary notion is that leaders can use religion and ritual to enhance their power because religion and ritual hide the true source of power from those over whom it is exercised. Maurice Godelier develops this idea with force, using data from the Inca Empire and present-day New Guinea (1977). In terms of Chinese society Albert Feuerwerker describes the function of 'ideology' in traditional China as 'a kind of cultural integument which protects the actual distribution of power and wealth from both direct apprehension by those who are ruled and from frontal attack' (1975: 57). Similarly, Stephan Feuchtwang argues that the ideology of Chinese society protects those in authority, in particular by playing up those aspects of the social system that appear to serve the interests of the governed: Chinese ideological structures 'serve to reproduce the relations of patronage and protection which ensured the forms of domination by a leisure class' (1975: 80).

In this chapter and the next, I propose to consider the general issues these analysts raise by addressing the following three questions in terms of traditional Chinese society:

(1) How might the religious and ritual system have been perceived to serve or have served the ends of government officials? (Chapter 6)

(2) How might the religious and ritual system have been perceived to threaten or have threatened the authority of government officials? (Chapter 6)

(3) How might the religious and ritual system have been perceived to serve or have served the ends of citizens outside officialdom? (Chapter 7)

My conclusions will be threefold. First, I agree with Bloch, Rappaport, Godelier, Feuerwerker, and Feuchtwang that Chinese religion and ritual may have served the ends of government officials in important ways. Second, to qualify my agreement with them, I argue that religion and ritual in the hands of those outside officialdom could have threatened the authority of officials in other ways. Third, to qualify my agreement still further, I argue in the next chapter that Chinese religion and ritual, particularly as practiced by peasants, could have served the interests of those subject to imperial power. Rather than seeing Chinese religion and ritual in the way Feuerwerker and Feuchtwang do, as a kind of smoked glass concealing the nature of power from those subject to it, I will suggest that peasant religion and ritual in China could have served as a magnifying glass on the nature of politics itself, revealing rather than concealing important information.

My conclusions ally me generally with analysts who agree that some rituals can reflect an accurate view of a society from the perspective of those at the bottom of it: Bourdillon (1978: 597), who has argued that ritual can be regarded as a challenge to existing hierarchies; Eva Hunt (1977: 131), who has argued that ceremonies surrounding voting in Mexico reveal a distinctly Indian view of hierarchy; and James Scott (1976: 231–3; 1977), who has argued that peasant ritual and religious belief often include a clear view of how peasants are exploited and a wishful view of an 'alternative moral universe' in which existing inequalities would be redressed.

Before addressing the three questions, I must comment on some ways the discussion will be limited. The dichotomy between government officials and citizens outside officialdom presupposed in the questions is greatly oversimplified. In actuality there are many intermediate points on a continuum. In the Ch'ing they included holders of degrees eligible for, but not presently in, office, holders of the *sheng-yüan* degree, who were regarded as local elite by common people but who were not eligible for office, and members of lineages who did not hold office, but whose kinsmen (close or distant) did. The continuum in post-1945 Taiwan is different in some respects. Political office is obtained by election, at least at lower levels, and eligibility is more closely connected with standing in the Kuomintang than with education. The cleavage between those in office and those outside is increased by the dominance of mainlanders (those who fled the mainland in 1945) in national political affairs.

In addition, there are differences in perspective even among those relatively unconnected to official authority: women, for example, usually have fewer jural rights and less authority in the family than men, quite apart from their lack of involvement in the political sphere.[1] However, to keep the discussion to a manageable size, I will consider only two points on the continuum: those occupying political office in their capacity as keepers of law and peace, and those relatively removed from the concerns of political office who are relatively without immediate aspirations to enter office.

I refer in the three questions to 'the' Chinese religious and ritual system. The question whether all Chinese religious and ritual practices formed one system in some sense will not be central to my argument. Various positions on this issue are taken by Wolf and Freedman in *Religion and Ritual in Chinese Society* (Wolf, ed. 1974b). To their arguments we can now add new material: Stephan Feuchtwang has shown that the official religion, promulgated by the state and practiced by its officials, was organized differently and proceeded on the basis of different assumptions from popular religion (1977). The scope of my aims is more limited: most of what I have to say relates to popular religion, including those portions of it in which officials became involved.

(1) How might the religious and ritual system have been perceived to serve or have served the ends of government officials?

One suggestion is that by canonizing dedicated and law-abiding citizens and officials posthumously, the government could praise and reward conduct of which it approved (Hsiao 1960: 221) and at the same time make a popular cult part of the official religion (Feuchtwang 1977: 606). Numerous examples can be found in the official correspondence of the late Ch'ing dynasty.[2] In a memorial of 15 January 1877,

The Governor-General and Governor of Kiangsu jointly memorialize asking sanction for the erection of a memorial temple at T'ai-ts'ang in honour of the late Governor of Honan, Ts'ien Ting-ming, a native of that place, to commemorate his public services during the rebellion. As one of the notables of Kiangsu at the time of the irruption of the Taipings into the neighborhood of Shanghai, he was at the head of the provincial trainband organization, and he came forward in particular to urge the despatch of reinforcements toward the coast from the army of Tseng Kwoh-fan. To secure this end he procured five European steamers to bring troops down from Ngan-k'ing; and he rendered most active and efficient service in the enrolment of auxiliary forces and the raising of funds, etc. − at this time (*Peking Gazette* 5 January 1878: 10).

A reply was received from the Emperor (published, in fact, before the memorial):

Shen Pao-cheng, Governor-General of the Two Kiang, and Wu Yüan-ping, Governor of Kiangsu, having jointly memorialized requesting that a title of canonization be conferred on the deceased Governor of Honan, Ts'ien Ting-ming, and that a special temple be erected in honour of his memory, a decree is issued acceding to this request, in addition to the honours heretofore conferred (*Peking Gazette* 4 January 1878: 3).

It is impossible to say whether canonization of this sort actually encouraged citizens to be loyal or virtuous, but it seems reasonable to suppose that officials hoped it would: models provided by zealous soldiers, upright officials, or citizens who died defending their country would have had obvious value for the state.[3]

There is much evidence that once deities were canonized, officials encouraged fear and respect for them as representatives of traditional morality. Wang Hui-tsu, a private secretary to various prefects in the late eighteenth century, who wrote several administrative handbooks for officials, declared:

Gods are not supernatural themselves, but they act supernaturally on the minds of those who believe in them. Why then, what is the harm if local authorities enlarge upon and adapt this fear of the gods in order that people should become better and reform? Is this not the meaning of the Divine Way and of the established moral doctrine? (Balazs 1965: 63).

Similarly, in a case described by Yang, numerous stele inscriptions in a Chen-wu temple in Kwangtung province described the god's contributions to social order over several centuries (1451–1899): bandits were fought off, attacking rebels repelled, thieves brought to justice. One stele, clearly written from the point of view of an official, or at least a member of the local elite who identified with an official's interests, read:

The image of the god is made only of clay and wood. He utters no words for people to hear, and issues no commands to hold them in awe. Yet he can prevent brutal men from bullying others, and can cause the unscrupulous to fail in their plots. The god has indeed lived up to expectations in enforcing law among the people and warding off great calamities and misfortune. The people have good cause to worship him (Yang 1961: 154).

A later stele, in 1797, asserted the need for renovating the temple in order to 'inspire reverence and awe' for morality and law. Whether or not Yang's conclusion, that the worship of Chen-wu 'helped to uphold government and law and maintain the general morality of society', is justified, it seems clear that local elite and officials hoped it would have that effect.

In much the same way, Kuomintang support for Confucian temples in Taiwan might well be calculated to encourage the traditional values of loyalty and stability; state support for temples that are not products of local community organization might well be calculated to break down the ethnic consciousness of Taiwanese and increase their identification with the nation (Feuchtwang 1974c: 301).[4]

Aside from incentives provided by deliberate official canonization and support of deities, it is also possible that an ordinary citizen's chance of becoming a god on the basis of meritorious acts carried out in life acted as an incentive that served government interests. Although most of my Taiwan informants declared jokingly that no one was good enough to become a god anymore, they also acknowledged that one or two individuals who died recently have come to be regarded as gods. The best known is a man who made great profits in the coal-mining industry and spent his money generously on magnificent temples for the god *Kuan-ti.*

Ritual and political authorities

Although this kind of generosity would rightly be considered beyond anything ordinary people could aspire to, members of a spirit writing cult in central Taiwan regard becoming a god as a very realistic possibility (Seaman 1974: 160). Various villagers who died in the recent past have revealed themselves through spirit writing to be occupying posts as gods. The meritorious acts which are the basis of their achievement are ones which would obviously be approved by the state: such acts as building a bridge out of one's own income or being active in public affairs (pp. 97–8). In fact, the list of merits that cult members strive to achieve contains numerous astoundingly pro-state elements. Under the category 'loyalty', positive acts include 'paying national taxes in full' and 'being slain for one's country'; negative acts include 'avoiding national taxes' and 'revolting against the government' (pp. 59–60). Since this cult operates outside direct state surveillance (indeed in Taiwan such cults are usually somewhat under the shadow of its disapproval), its support of values and acts of obvious service to the state is all the more impressive.

To return to ways officials deliberately used belief in the gods, when they performed rituals entreating the gods' help in time of need, they may have been seeking to show, or may have succeeded in showing, citizens that the state had the people's welfare at heart (Hsiao 1960: 221). An edict of 1874 reads: 'The Emperor will in person, on the 9th of January, again proceed to the Temple of Heaven, to pray for snow. Several high princes are deputed to pray in other temples. Supplications to the same effect were made on 30th and 31st December, and a certain amount has fallen, but not enough for the requirements of the farmers' (*Peking Gazette* 5 January 1875: 2). Again it is impossible to say whether citizens interpreted these acts as motivated by concern for their plight. It seems fair to surmise that if they were not (though they may well have been) motivated by concern for the people's welfare, they were motivated by a desire to make people *think* the government was concerned about them.

As I have mentioned, Feuchtwang suggests that the religious system protected the government against threat by displaying disproportionately its beneficial aspects. This is related to a suggestion, made by Robin Horton, that in any given social setting the quality of the relationships between men and gods might serve to counterbalance the quality of the relationships among men. In a setting where men related affectionately to one another, they might relate impersonally to the gods, and vice versa (1960: 220). If this were so, and the Chinese political system could be described as 'oppressive' from a peasant's point of view, we might expect a peasant's religious system to be 'protective'. One argument in favor of its protectiveness can be made on the basis of material to be introduced below: whereas officials are difficult of access and shielded by intermediaries, many of whom are rapacious and corrupt, gods are easily accessible to anyone who directly addresses their images. One might argue further that whereas involvement in a magistrate's court would be assiduously avoided because of the enormous cost of customary fees at every step of the way, and the uncertainty of the

81

outcome, a god could be asked for help or advice at little cost and with nothing to lose; whereas the range of things officials would even consider dealing with was narrow (legal infringements, gross suffering as from a natural disaster) the gods would consider any request, concerning anything from a suitable mate for one's daughter to rain for one's crop. One would have to add that offerings to the gods might well be expensive and their cost felt burdensome; that although a god could be asked for anything, there was no way of knowing that he would grant it. But, in all, I would conclude that the gods are strikingly accessible and amenable to petition, compared to officials. This would be one way in which gods stress the more positive aspects of the political system (or even manufacture them) and so gives us a reason to accept Feuchtwang's claim.

Another suggestion is that by placing blame for misfortune on the gods, the government may have sought to strengthen its own legitimacy (Hsiao 1960: 221). The idea is that if flood, drought, or other natural disasters were blamed on the gods, officials could not be blamed for them. This notion is especially convincing when gods were reprimanded for failing to control natural phenomena (see p. 12 above). But the point cannot be argued wholeheartedly, because the gods brought natural disaster precisely when there was maladministration in the empire. Ultimate responsibility was thus returned to officials. In addition, making the gods responsible for certain natural events had its limitations: if the gods were beseeched for help, they had to be given credit when things improved. In the following imperial decree, the efforts of officials were recognized, but ultimate credit was reserved for the god.

A Decree in answer to a memorial by the Governor-General of the Yellow River, reporting the safety of both banks of the river at the setting in of late Autumn, when no further rise of the water is to be apprehended, the emergencies which have occurred at various points since last spring having been successfully met by the exertions of the Governor-General and the officials of his staff. For the divine protection to which this safety is due, his Majesty feels reverently grateful; and he commands that ten sticks of Tibetan incense be sent to the Governor-General, to be offered on the Imperial behalf of the temple of the God of the River (*Peking Gazette* 7 November 1875: 119).

However, it might be misleading to describe the preceding case as if it mitigated official power. For it is extremely important to recognize that the emperor decided when and if honors and thanks were to be bestowed on lower gods. He delegated credit to gods as he did to his subordinate officials. The following case illustrates the point.

The acting Governor of Shantung memorializes soliciting an acknowledgement of the divine protection afforded by the presiding spirit of the Yellow River. It was requested last year, by the Governor Ting Pao-cheng, in consequence of the aid supernaturally manifested on diverse occasions on behalf of the embankment works at Kun Ch'eng by the great Prince Li (the canonized spirit of a former Governor-General of the Yellow River, named Li Yü-mei), that an honorific title be Imperially conferred upon this divinity, and that he be included for purposes of worship within the temple of the Four Great Golden Dragon Princes. The latter portion of this request was acceded to, on confirmation by the Board of Ceremonies, in suspense pending further manifestations of divine response in time of need. The Governor now reports that in the sixth moon of the present year, when officials were employed under his orders in attending to the safety of the embankments, the waters of the river became swollen, and a time of danger presented itself at the confluence of the Tai Ho. The banks appeared as though shaken, and a day and a night were spent in labours of repair without ensuring safety. It was not until the following day, when [the effigy] of the Four Great Golden Dragons and of the Great Prince Li were brought to the scene of the works, that the current abated its force, and the abutments were securely strengthened. [Three other instances of the god's aid are described here.] These repeated instances of divine interposition are considered sufficient to warrant the bestowal of a title of honour. – Rescript: Let the Board of Ceremonies consider and report (*Peking Gazette* 7 December 1875: 132).

In the Republican government of Taiwan, the institution of conferring honors on gods has continued to be the prerogative of high political authorities (Feuchtwang 1974c: 281).

Finally, one could argue that the religious system did not open the possibility of a more even distribution of power and resources: it posed no alternative to the allocation of power in the traditional class system. It never questioned whether powerful figures should sit in judgement over and dole out favors to ordinary people; it almost invariably saw the source of power over other people and valued resources emanating from a bureaucratic hierarchy modeled on the actual government. As Arthur Wolf has pointed out, when revolutionary movements did arise in China, they avoided the traditional gods, utilizing instead the images of foreign traditions such as Buddhism and Christianity (1964a: 145). In this sense the spiritual realm may have worked to the advantage of those who ruled: the world of spirits did not open the possibility of a radically different kind of world.

(2) How might the religious and ritual system have been perceived to threaten or have threatened the authority of government officials?

We have seen in discussing (1) that the government had a lively interest in delegating rights and honors to spirits: provincial officials memorialized the throne to ask permission for a god's sacrifices to be included in the official roster, for his temple to be rebuilt or for an honor to be bestowed on him. Ch'ing law stipulated that private erection of temples and convents was prohibited and set down punishments for any Buddhist or Taoist priest who did so or any official who failed to prohibit it (Yang 1961: 187). Outside the imperially sanctioned area, there was, of course, a wealth of other religious and ritual activity, some of which was tolerated and some of which was not. Despite the law, private construction of temples and worship in them were evidently widely tolerated, as long as they appeared harmless (Hsiao 1960: 229). At the beginning of the Ch'ing dynasty in the seventeenth century, only 16 per cent of the temples listed in the official statistics were built with imperial permission (Yang 1961: 188). One local gazetteer from Ho Hsien described the people's preference for non-official temples:

If houses of worship are to be built or repaired, the larger ones of which entail an expense of a thousand taels and smaller ones several hundred, so many persons make contributions that the work is accomplished easily . . . But when Confucian temples that have to do with sustaining good morals [are to be built or repaired], nobody cares even to ask a question [concerning the matter] (Hsiao 1960: 221).

The existence of gods who were not officially recognized could lead to direct confrontations between the strength of popular cults and the strength or determination of official opposition. In time of great need the people might attempt to draw local officials into the worship of a god whose efficacy they respected but who was not officially recognized. Their hope would be that an official's prayers would exercise special influence on his colleague in the spiritual realm. The official was forbidden by law to worship any deity not on the official lists, but he risked widespread popular disapproval and disturbance if he refused (Ch'ü 1962: 165). Doolittle reports a case in which a magistrate sometimes did as requested.

Sometimes the procession, while thus praying for rain, takes the liberty of entering one of the court-yards attached to the various mandarin official residences, where they beat the drums and the gong until they are pleased to depart. Some assert that occasionally the mandarin thus called upon condescends to present himself before the rabble, in which case the monster image of the Dragon King is placed before a table. He then returns to his apartments. The bearer of the Dragon King soon after places the image over his shoulders, and the procession takes its departure (Doolittle 1966: II, 118).

Officials participate in local cults in Taiwan today, sponsoring local festivals and holding ritual offices, precisely in order to increase their legitimacy. 'In the eyes of many common people ritual offices seem to grant legitimacy and authority to men whose association with the Kuomintang and offices in the state administrative structure gives them only power' (DeGlopper 1973: 93).

In other cases officials refused to participate. In 1789 in Ning-yüan, Hunan, the local people brought about twenty images of village gods to the yamen, requesting permission to bring them into the great hall of audience, so that Wang Hui-tsu, the official, could bow before them and pray for rain. His speech to them ended with the statement:

The Rites do not allow for the magistrate to bow and pray. It is not that I do not love the people, but it is impossible to act contrary to the canon of the Rites or to offend against the statutes of the State. So return home quickly with your gods! If you meet relatives and friends on your way, tell them of my words, and do not try to enter the city again (Balazs 1965: 64).

Even if some officials would accede to the people's request to pay homage to local gods, others, quite reasonably, perceived such requests as a threat to governmental law and authority.[5]

Although the building of officially unsanctioned temples may have been ignored, ritual activities focused on those temples were less likely to be ignored, especially if they involved the gathering or movement of large masses of people, or the propagation of noncanonical writings. The Ch'ing code included a statute providing a punishment of one hundred blows of the heavy bamboo for the chief organizer of a religious procession (Bodde and Morris 1967: 273). Although the statute was probably largely ignored, it points out the government's uneasiness about large groups of people gathering for some ritual purpose not sanctioned (or led) by government officials. As we will see below, this was probably in part a result of fear that heretical and explicitly anti-dynastic sects might emerge from such activity, but it may well have also resulted from understandable unease, on the part of those (relatively few) in governmental office, over the potential strength of the masses they governed when that potential strength was manifested in crowd activity. To this point, a Ch'ing proclamation against processing gods explicitly forbids the assembly of 'crowds for religious purpose' (Allen 1872c: 517).

What Taiwanese villagers value as *lau-ziat* (bustling, warm, human activity) their officials even today disapprove. Officials on Taiwan explain their disapproval by saying the festivals waste money. But the legal measures they have adopted against them (restricting the number of villages that can *pai-pai* on the same day and the number of households that can bring their offerings to the main temple) must at least in part be intended to prevent the gathering of enormous masses of people. It does not require much imagination to see why any (coercive) government might prefer not to see huge crowds engaged in organized activities it had not sanctioned.[6]

It is even easier to understand why large crowds moving out of their local areas would have been regarded with disapproval. Hsiao cites an edict of 1739 written by the Ch'ien-lung emperor:

During the first and second months of the year, hundreds of thousands of people gather in groups [for the pilgrimage]. They first go to the *ch'eng-huang* temple of the provincial city where they burn incense and a letter of invocation, calling the procedure 'registration'. Then they begin their journey, going in various directions . . . Men and women mix promiscuously, and it is impossible to tell the good from the bad. Fights, kidnapping, and thievery occur, and other incidents crop up in the dark. Such a vile practice constitutes at present a waste of money and is liable to give rise to heretical sects in the future (Hsiao 1960: 230).

In addition to the reasons the emperor cites, one might add the desire to prohibit such a show of potential strength in numbers.

More categorically outlawed and more assiduously suppressed were organized sects that met secretly or possessed secret signals, largely because, as we have seen, such sects were often explicitly anti-dynastic (Chesneaux 1971: 75–9;

Yang 1961: 192–8). Here I will only discuss one aspect of surveillance over secret societies, because it relates to our earlier discussion of charms. The writing of charms was singled out for special mention in the legal articles against secret sects (Yang 1961: 204). In addition 'noncanonical' magical writings and spells were separately named in the legal code.

The governor of Shensi has reported a case in which a Buddhist monk, Ni Tao-yüan, when his former disciple had returned from an itinerant tour bearing non-canonical magical writings, not only failed to report them immediately to the authorities but even lent a hand to their copying and propagation.

By analogy to the statute . . . providing deportation for one who fabricates magical writings and spells without, however, reaching large numbers of people, Ni Tao-yüan is to receive a one-degree lesser sentence, namely 100 blows of the heavy bamboo and three years penal servitude (Bodde and Morris 1967: 289). [The penalty for reaching large numbers of people was decapitation after the assizes.]

If religious festivals were disliked in part because they allowed a show of numerical strength, charms (which, as we have seen, were orders or mandates) may have been disliked in part because they might call for action or response on demand of a non-official authority. If that authority became identified with an organization dedicated to overthrowing the state, the charm could appear a threatening weapon indeed.[7]

This discussion of whether ritual helps or hinders the ends of political authorities can be pushed in the direction of more specific hypotheses if we return to the subject of Chapter 4, divination. This will allow me to relate constitutive rules and restricted codes to the realm of politics, and at the same time, to suggest that rituals of divination that involve restricted codes are more useful to political authorities than those that do not.

Many writers have pointed out in a general way the important relation between divinatory systems and sources of authority.[8] Park has noted that 'divinatory procedure has the effect of stamping with a mark of special legitimacy a particular decision or a particular kind of response to crisis' (1963: 200). Fortes identifies the source of this legitimacy for the Tallensi case in the 'ultimate authority' of the ancestors: 'A confirmed divinatory verdict is an authorization, a sanction emanating from the ultimate source of authority in matters that concern the occult, the occult agencies themselves, for the ritual action proposed' (1966: 415). Bascom identifies one source of legitimacy for the Yoruba case as the authority of the god (Ifa) who controls the outcome and, in part, the content of the messages he sends. These verses

generally follow the pattern of describing a previous divination, for an animal or legendary character, which is to serve as a precedent for the client; they begin by naming the diviner who made the prediction and usually tell the problem that confronted the character and the sacrifice that was prescribed for him. They tell how that character either sacrificed and prospered, or failed to sacrifice and met with misfortune, and conclude by stating or implying that the present client is confronted by a similar problem and should make similar sacrifice (1941: 43).

Actions proven efficacious by past experience are cited as precedent in the present.

Chinese divination shared this authoritativeness: any divination involving communication with the gods was invested with their authority. Some oracle slips used in *thiu-chiam* cited precedent, much in the fashion of Yoruba oracles, and some referred to historical events: 'In former times [the scholar] Chi-tzu was journeying to Ch'in. He had attained no distinction, and had returned to Lo-yang. One day the roll of successful candidates bore his name, and he returned home, the bearer of the golden seals of the six countries' (Allen 1872b: 507). Sometimes, as Eberhard has discovered, they referred to events in historical dramas, many of which were familiar to those who consulted the oracle (1970: 194–8). Otherwise, they might well cite moral tenets that clearly belonged to traditional morality:[9] 'Heaven is propitious or the reverse according to your deserts. If you are true and sincere in your worship, every thing you pray for shall be granted you; for I am pretty sure you are faithful to the duties of relationship' (Allen 1872a: 505).

To see more precise relationships between divinatory systems and political authorities, let us turn to Maurice Bloch's cogent argument that formalization in political oratory and ritual song and dance is a means of social control. Through formalization, what can be said is restricted: 'choice of form, of style, of words and of syntax is less than in ordinary language' (1974: 60). In political oratory, formalization can be made to serve the ends of superiors:

If a superior addresses an inferior, the latter, if he accepts to answer within the formalised code imposed on the situation (and he will rarely be in a position to do anything else) will find himself in a position where he cannot say 'no' . . . It is because the formalisation of language is a way whereby one speaker can coerce the response of another that it can be seen as a form of social control (1974: 63, 64).

Although the particular analysis Bloch makes of Merina oratory would be difficult to apply, point by point, to Chinese divination, his analysis leads us directly to the question whether there is any relationship between the form of different divinatory acts and the exercise of authority. Let us consider an extremely restricted form of divination (*thiu-chiam*) on the one hand, and a much less restricted form (spirit possession) on the other, and in both cases let us consider the perspective of those outside formal positions of political power and those inside such positions.

From the perspective of an ordinary citizen consulting the gods, the restricted nature of *thiu-chiam* might have enhanced its authority: the total set of possible replies was enshrined in tradition and the method by which replies were obtained was relatively safe from human fraud. One could also argue, in a fashion analogous to Bloch, that the prescribed nature of the moves in a consultation was a means of control: the petitioner *must* first throw the *pue*, then draw a stick, then throw *pue* again and so on. One would have to add, as Bloch realizes, that this control worked both ways: the petitioner could be virtually certain of getting a reply of *some* kind from the god. A more likely way in which the restriction of the code used might have operated to enhance authority comes from the form-letter-like standardization of the replies. I do not know whether, just as we feel distance between bureaucratic authorities and ourselves on receipt of a standardized reply (distance which is a function of their license to disregard us as individuals because of their superior position), so Chinese petitioners felt something similar. In any case, they would have been very likely to regard such treatment as appropriate from a being so superior in authority (and so busy with other important affairs).

As if to clinch this point, Ch'ing bureaucrats, like gods, used standardized messages, and many of them were called by precisely the same name as divination slips: *chiam* (Mandarin *ch'ien*). A '*he-chiam*' (urgent warrant) was given to mandarins' messengers as proof of the special urgency of their commands (Douglas 1873: 77). The phrase '*ch'u-ch'ien*' meant 'to issue warrant or order – as done in open court by the presiding official drawing the requisite "slip" from the bamboo tube before him, and flinging it to one of his lictors for immediate execution' (Giles 1912: I, 208).[10] Huc gives us a description:

The Prefect took up from the table a piece of bamboo wood, and threw it into the middle of the court. A figure was marked upon it, which pointed out the number of blows the prisoner was to receive. One of the executioners picked it up, examined the figure, and cried, in a chanting tone, 'Fifteen blows'; that is to say, the criminal would receive thirty – for the executioners always double the number ordered by the judge – and this, multiplied by the number of executioners, furnished a frightful total (1970: II, 249–50).

In effect, then, the details of the method magistrates used to communicate in court were very similar to the details of the method gods used to communicate in temples: the apparatus of issuing a warrant was virtually the same as the apparatus of issuing a lot in *thiu-chiam* divination. (See above, p. 47.)[11] This parallel alone, assuming people were aware of it, might well have enhanced the authority of gods who communicated in this way.

From the perspective of those in positions of formal authority *thiu-chiam* divination would have probably appeared to be one of the least threatening activities involving the gods. The messages were public, accessible to anyone who wished to read them; they were also politically neutral, citing historical events or moral maxims in the general texts and relating these to personal concerns in the particular categories. This is not to say that messages *could not* have been given a political reading, but only that the system did not predispose itself to this. 'Rebellion' was not one of the categories about which one could ask. What is more, the set of messages was not extendible; this part of the practice was closed and frozen in shape. The number or content of the messages could not have been changed without a deliberate decision being made by relevant authorities, probably on direct instruction from the gods, perhaps via a medium. In this case the relevant authorities would probably have been a temple committee, often composed of local elite, people who would surely have been involved in furthering their own advance through the state bureaucracy and thus unlikely to have subverted it.

Less restricted forms of divination, such as those involving spirit possession, were differently related to authority. As far as ordinary citizens were concerned, a spirit-medium might speak with greater or lesser authority than a *chiam*. Because of the constant possibility of false possession or pretended possession, mediums in Taiwan are often treated with great skepticism, treatment which robs their pronouncements of legitimacy. However, if they are regarded as genuine, they can exercise authority in a much more dramatic fashion than a *chiam*. The procedure of inducing possession and dealing with a god once he has possessed a man is far less restricted by rules than *thiu-chiam*, but the god can order, direct, command, and express displeasure or anger very dramatically, and thus quite effectively compel respect for his authority.[12]

From the point of view of those in formal authority, the pronouncements of mediums and oracles must have appeared singularly controllable. Their messages were unpredictable, changeable, and might have been directed to any subject whatsoever: the practice was open. In the following cases, oracles served the purposes of established authority. One concerns a temple of the god of learning:

On one of the beams which support the roof is a brazen eagle, from the bill of which a long cord hangs in front of the altar. Attached to the cord is a pencil with which the deity is supposed to write mystic scrolls on a table covered with sand, or, as others say, upon sheets of paper placed on the table. These written oracles, the productions of crafty priesthood, are generally announcements of impending calamities, and are forwarded to the authorities in order that they may adopt precautionary measures. In 1853, when Kwang-tung was overrun with rebels, a communication of this nature was forwarded to the governor-general of the province. It called upon the people to eschew rebellion as one of the greatest crimes, and Yeh, who was then governor-general, embodied the oracle in a proclamation, which was posted in the crowded thoroughfares of Canton and its suburbs (Gray 1878: II, 145).

The other concerns a temple of General Liu-meng, the god of insects (in Kiangsu):

During the celebration of the god's birthday, thousands of peasants collected on the temple grounds to see the procession. One year, the bridge at the side of the temple was about to collapse, and repair work was not completed by the celebration date. The county magistrate ordered that there be no procession in order to prevent crowds from gathering on the bridge. The peasants angrily refused to obey. The magistrate was about to go out personally to pacify the crowd when he received a report that the whole issue had been settled. One of the community leaders had performed divination with the planchette, and had told the peasants that the god advised stopping the procession for that year on account of the danger of the dilapidated bridge. The peasants accepted the decision without further question. Thus the voice of the gods stopped a threatened riot when the voice of the law and authority had failed (Yang 1961: 261).

But the authorities must have realized full well that these forms of spirit possession could as easily have worked against their interests. Some official decrees specifically denounced spirit-mediums, but it is hard to know whether they did so because mediums were regarded as uncontrollable, fraudulent, or unseemly (particularly in the case of female mediums) (De Groot 1970: 20).

Spirit *writing* might have appeared somewhat more amenable to control by established authorities than spirit-*mediums*. For the simple reason that written messages must be read by the literate (most of whom would have had some exposure to classical learning and presumably some commitment or even aspiration to the official bureaucracy), communications made in this form must have been potentially more open to scrutiny. In Amoy, many spirit associations counted literary and official men among their numbers. 'People of the best classes, and even higher officials' sought oracles from certain temples in great numbers (De Groot 1969: VI, 1297).

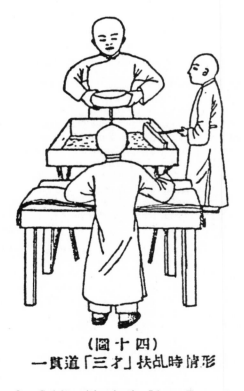

（圖 十 四）
一貫道「三才」扶乩時情形

9   Spirit writing in the *I-kuan Tao* sect

Ritual and political authorities

As in the case of spirit-mediums, spirit writing could sometimes benefit officials. A communication received from *Kuan-ti* (a god who was part of the official pantheon) during a plague in Hong Kong guaranteed that the plague should last no longer than half a year and that no more than 5,000 families should be struck. Further, it assured that 'no dwelling where filial devotion and friendship prevail will be entered by any plague demons' (De Groot 1969: I, 302–5). *Kuan-ti* spoke 'by appointment of the Great Imperial Ch'ing dynasty' much as one might imagine an earthly magistrate speaking, to calm people's fears and avert panic.

At the same time, it is significant that some secret societies (all of which were uncompromisingly outlawed by the Ch'ing penal code) focused on spirit writing (Chesneaux 1971: 75; Deliusin 1972: 229; Grootaers 1951). Although the specific content of the messages they received may have been heavily Confucian, their effect was to validate the sect's teachings (many advocating rebellion against the state) as a whole.[13]

This material suggests the hypothesis that in China formally restricted sorts of divination (which are relatively closed practices) are less likely to be seen as interfering with the functions of established authority than unrestricted sorts (which are relatively open practices). Additional questions that need exploration are whether closed forms of divination persisted because Chinese authorities overtly encouraged them, or whether they persisted simply because, in the perception of ordinary people who used these cults, their ossification, standardization, and somewhat arbitrary application to individuals accurately reflected the nature of formal authority in everyday life.

7

Ritual as a learning game

While I have argued that Chinese political authorities could use religion and ritual to enhance their power over citizens, I have also argued that citizens could use religion and ritual to oppose political authorities. Further insight into how religion and ritual could have served the ends of ordinary citizens will come from consideration of the third question set out at the beginning of Part III.

(3) How might the religious and ritual system have been perceived to serve or have served the ends of citizens outside officialdom? In focusing on features of ritual communications with spirits that make them amenable to the ends of those outside positions of official authority, I am taking a stand opposed to that of Bloch, Feuerwerker, Feuchtwang, Godelier, and Rappaport as described at the beginning of Chapter 6. They argue that ritual conceals the true nature of authority from the ruled, thus enhancing the position of rulers. In contrast, I will argue below that the Chinese religious and ritual system may have served a teaching function for peasants, illustrating vividly, frequently, and in a variety of contexts how one got power, how one got access to those with power, and how one limited those with power.[1] I will suggest that one important thing Chinese peasants were learning in manipulating the rules and practices of their religious system, was how to analyze (and so manipulate) the political system that governed them.

Before moving to this argument, it is necessary to ask whether the ritual and religious system could be seen as a kind of social theory in which the workings of the political order were skillfully analyzed from the people's point of view. To this end I will take up some features of the government bureaucracy, showing what the religious system had to say about them. I have deliberately chosen features with some degree of abstraction whose presence in the religious system would indicate an analytic understanding. We will see that the religious system mirrored the bureaucratic political system with uncanny sociological accuracy.

Office

Some gods were explicitly said to occupy an office. As one Ch'inan villager put

92

it, 'There are all kinds of *Tho-te-kong* — of mountains, of fields, of bridges, of houses, of temples — governing a certain area. They are all different: the posts are all filled by different men who did good deeds while they were alive. If one sets up a new statue of *Tho-te-kong* in one's house, another god will come to fill the *Tho-te-kong* post.'

Not everyone would agree with this statement, however, and there were sometimes arguments about in what sense all *Tho-te-kong* are the same. One man argued that all *Tho-te-kong* serve the same protective function, but that there is only one spirit — a particular individual who was given this responsibility after his death. Others explained that various *Tho-te-kong* images are like photographs of the same man. Sometimes people obviously took one position or another out of special interests; a member of the tightly knit Ui lineage who lived in the lineage community claimed that their *Tho-te-kong* had a different incumbent from the village-wide (Ch'inan) one, thus stressing the lineage's separate identity. A member of the same lineage who lived some distance away from the community insisted that all *Tho-te-kong* (including the nearby one he worshipped) were the same spirit, thus stressing his identity with the lineage even though he lived apart from it. But through it all, the notion of office, with its attendant responsibilities, was being utilized. People only disagreed over whether the office had one incumbent or many.[2]

There was more agreement when more powerful gods were discussed. *Co-su-kong* is like the Ch'ing emperor, I was told: there is only one of him. One man said *Thi:-kong* (the highest god) is an office that is now being filled by a particular god, *Kuan-ti*, and many others compared *Thi:-kong* to Taiwan's president. The point of all these comparisons was to say that *this* office has only one incumbent. As one moves up in the hierarchy of power, one reaches the apex of a pyramid: there are fewer offices and fewer incumbents as one approaches the top. The religious hierarchy neatly captures this aspect of the government hierarchy.

Hierarchy

We have already discussed in detail many of the ways hierarchy was recognized and expressed in the religious system: food and ritual money offerings were graded according to the spirits' rank; verbal and gestural forms of etiquette were observed according to relative rank; restricted codes marked distance between petitioners and spirits.[3]

Authority appropriate to rank

Understanding of this notion is fundamental to manipulation of the religious system. Gods were implored to control ghosts by virtue of their authority over them; gods delegated their greater authority to Taoist priests and ordinary people by issuing sealed charms; gods of intermediate authority could be asked to intercede with gods of high authority on behalf of persons who did not wish to approach them directly (see p. 22 above); an official of high authority could be asked to instruct a subordinate god not to neglect his responsibilities.

Means by which officials obtained and transferred information

All major means were commonplace in the ritual system: writing, tours, and audiences. As we have seen, memorials, contracts, and bills of transfer of goods were sent from men to spirits; orders, edicts, and proclamations moved from spirits to men. Both gods and officials made regular tours of their territories; both gods and officials (the former to a much less restricted extent) permitted audiences so that subordinates could speak to them.

Source of superordinates' power and authority

As we have discussed, values dear to the state — loyalty to family or country — were played out in the personal histories of many gods. But peasants were far from blinded by official encouragement of these virtues: morally wicked men and social rebels could become gods as well (Hamberg 1935: 36). The power to respond to requests and make things happen (being *lieng*) was the ultimate criterion of a spirit's becoming a god. In this respect the villagers' religion gives us a startling view of the system from the bottom up: some of my Taiwanese informants were able to articulate a meaning of *lieng* beyond that of 'responsiveness'. They said a god is *lieng* when many people *say* he is; *lieng* is a result of popularity and allegiance from the people.[4]

When we say a god is *lieng* we mean the god really does help us. Word is then spread from person to person, each telling the other that the god helped. So it is really a matter of relations among men . . . A change in the popularity of temples is not a result of change in the gods' abilities. The abilities of gods don't change. People's attitudes toward them do, however.

In the government's view, the gods' authority was delegated from above as they were admitted into the official lists and given honors and titles (or in Taiwan simply approval); in the people's view the gods' power was generated from below. This notion of the 'mandate of the people' was articulate with respect to the gods, and at least at times was also recognized with respect to the officials. It would surely not be too far-fetched to suggest that it was general knowledge that if widespread (and well-founded) popular dissatisfaction with a local official's conduct could be made known to higher authorities, he might well be prevented from taking office or removed from it. 'There were instances in which the people prevented officials with reputations as oppressors from taking office, or upbraided those in office in scurrilous placards. In other instances, inhabitants of county seats punished unjust officials after they had left office by barring the city gates, beating up the official's servants, and stripping the clothes off his female relatives' (Watt 1977: 383).

Limits on a superordinate's power and authority

Here we continue to see the system from the bottom up: we have seen that temples could decline in popularity and even be abandoned if the god were no longer thought *lieng*. It seems doubtful whether people would routinely conclude that an official who was removed from office because of misconduct was removed as a result of popular disapproval. But it seems possible that people recognized this as a *potential* means by which a corrupt or incompetent official could be removed.

Specialization of government personnel

Although in Weber's view a bureaucratic system was marked by a 'systematic division of labor', it has been argued that the Chinese state bureaucracy was largely made up of generalists: for example, each district magistrate was responsible for the same range of tasks, from law enforcement to tax collection (Watt 1977: 374; Weber 1947: 330; Yang 1959: 134—46). This feature was reflected in the nature of gods' activities. Although some might be said to have special talents, largely all were competent in the same range of things. The list of topics one can ask about in *puaq-pue* divination is remarkably similar even in temples as far apart as Taiwan and the New Territories.[5]

Uniformity of procedures and rules

In Weber's formal analysis, a bureaucrat operated according to a body of legal rules that were to be uniformly applied to particular cases (Weber 1947: 330; Blau 1974: 30). There were many Ch'ing bureaucrats who urged that formal rules should be the primary basis for administration. An extensive body of legal codes and administrative rules existed for the guidance of officials: the codes specified punishments for various sorts of crimes and misdemeanors, and the rules specified how an official should conduct his affairs (Yang 1959: 146–7).

This feature is found in some rituals. The uniformity of divination procedures is like the uniformity of procedures citizens use in dealing with officials. A majority of temples I inquired about in northern Taiwan use the same system of lots (*thiu-chiam*) described above. Interpretations of the fall of *pue* are also widely uniform, given certain limited variations. In the gods' dealings with men, I have suggested that the set categories of question and response in *thiu-chiam* divination are like form-letter replies: the infinite particulars of each person's situation are lost when they are classed into a strictly limited set of possibilities.[6]

95

Impersonality of officials

In Weber's analysis, the person in office 'is subject to an impersonal order to which his actions are oriented' (1947: 330). Much has been written on the difficulties Chinese officials had in applying laws and following procedures impersonally. Despite extensive legal precautions, ties of kinship and friendship often intruded (Yang 1959: 156ff.). Some aspects of the ritual system seem to presuppose impersonal, impartial superordinates: a petitioner identifies himself in Taiwan only by his name and address and not by reference to his kinsmen's deeds of piety; most temples are open places, to which any person has access, regardless of family or other connections. Other aspects point to superordinates with whom it is possible to build special relationships. People's statements that it is necessary to show respect to the gods frequently (to have *ong-lai*) before they will help might be relevant. In addition, in Ch'ing China and Taiwan today, all kinds of specialized groups could have their own images of gods or pay particular attention to certain gods: clans, lineages, occupational groups such as merchants, taxi-drivers, actors, coal-miners, or students. These are ways in which the gods — and by analogy officials — could be persuaded to pay special attention to particular groups or individuals.

The conclusion seems to me inescapable that Chinese peasants knew an astonishing amount about the bureaucracy that governed them. We can now address the suggestion made above, that the Chinese religious and ritual system served a teaching function in which peasants learned about their government. It is always difficult to produce direct evidence that a social institution serves a certain function. Therefore I shall approach the problem obliquely. Here are two preliminary points. First, if the ritual system did have this function why would it have been useful? Aside from the obvious point that accurate knowledge of how a system of authority works is always useful when dealing with it, there is the point that the state system worked at least in part on principles that were largely foreign to the local and kinship groups people lived in. As Yang put it: 'Traditional China may be thought of as having two major structural components: a national bureaucratic superstructure emphasizing centralization, standardization, formalism, a monocratically organized hierarchy of authority, and the norm of impersonality; and a vast substratum of heterogeneous local communities based on a morally oriented social order and the informal primary group' (1959: 135).

In another context Fallers has suggested that when authorities introduce a bureaucratic civil service into a society with a particularistic traditional authority structure (as the British did for the African Busoga), numerous conflicts arise (1969: 441–9). Similarly, in the Chinese case there are many conflicts between the bureaucratic central government and the particularistic traditional authority of local communities, and I would hasten to say I am not arguing that the ritual system ameliorated conflict as such. I would only suggest that if it indeed displayed for people — taught them about — the principles underlying the operation of their powerful central government, it would have done a useful thing.

Second, even if the ritual system had this function, in what way was it limited? The most important way, though there are others, is that it could not have shown people how to overthrow the existing government and substitute for it a radically different kind of political organization. Marx and Engels said that the ruling ideas of every age are the ideas of the ruling class (1970: 64—8). Chinese religion, mirroring the system of state control as closely as it did, could scarcely have shown a way out from under it, though it might, as I will suggest shortly, have shown people how to escape the oppression of a particular incumbent. In other words, the religious system could well have shown people how to operate within the existing system. Something was concealed, as Feuerwerker and Feuchtwang have said, but something was also revealed.

I would suggest it is possible that the formal similarities between the Chinese religious system and the political system made the one an apt tool for understanding the workings of the other. If dealing with the gods could be seen as a rehearsal, or playing out, of skills important in dealing with the earthly power system, this gives us one way of understanding why interactions with gods were fashioned in such detail after ordinary interactions. The more detailed the rehearsal, the more likely the real performance is to succeed.

One aspect of the rules that operate in closed ritual practices — that they are limited — is relevant here. By limiting the rules (and thus the factors one need consider) one simplifies a situation artificially. As we have seen, there are certain occasions when simplified sets of rules (restricted codes) are useful. Another of these is learning games. A child playing with Cuisenaire rods needs only attend to the color and relative length of the rods: names of numbers are ruled out, explicitly to simplify the process of learning mathematics. In a similar fashion, the set of Chinese ritual practices that were restricted might facilitate perception of important aspects of the analogous government system by limiting what one had to attend to. For example, methods of divination using restricted codes stress invariant procedures and require that general replies be interpreted in the light of individual cases. Attention would be focused on skills involved in these activities, skills that would obviously be of use in dealing with officials.

Mention of 'focusing attention' leads us to consider the role of metaphor itself in all this. Max Black has suggested that metaphor functions by focusing our attention on some limited aspects of a resemblance between two things. He suggests:

Suppose I look at the night sky through a piece of heavily smoked glass on which certain lines have been left clear. Then I shall see only the stars that can be made to lie on the lines previously prepared upon the screen, and the stars I do see will be seen as organized by the screen's structure. We can think of a metaphor as such a screen and the system of 'associated commonplaces' of the focal word as the network of lines upon the screen. We can say that the principal subject is 'seen through' the metaphorical expression — or, if we prefer, that the principal subject is 'projected upon' the field of the subsidiary subject' (1962: 41).

In terms of a particular analogy:

Suppose I am set the task of describing a battle in words drawn as largely as possible from the vocabulary of chess. These latter terms determine a system of implications which will proceed to control my description of the battle. The enforced choice of the chess vocabulary will lead some aspects of the battle to be emphasized, others to be neglected, and all to be organized in a way that would cause much more strain in other modes of description. The chess vocabulary filters and transforms: it not only selects, it brings forward aspects of the battle that might not be seen at all through another medium (1962: 41—2).

In the Chinese case, the metaphor might be stated as, 'Gods are officials', or, 'The spiritual world is a bureaucracy'. The 'associated commonplaces' about the nature of gods and their bureaucracy shape and selectively emphasize the world of officials. But if I am to suggest that the religious system had some kind of teaching function, I must press one step further, and say that seeing the state system through the metaphor of the ritual system elucidated and clarified the state system.[7]

This claim would be more plausible if we found that the ritual system used by ordinary citizens focused attention on those aspects of the government that citizens would be likely to notice and be concerned about. For example, one might expect ordinary citizens to notice ways that the power of the state was limited, and the ritual system seems to stress these. It stresses: the obligation of those in power to those beneath them, lest the loyalty of those under them, the very basis of their power, be removed; the moveable nature of official personnel, such that new gods who served the people's needs were continually created, and old ones who did not were forgotten; the contingent nature of allegiance, such that payment for a request was withheld until the request was granted.

In parallel fashion, we might expect the ritual system of other sectors of society (that of officials, for example) to present us with a different picture. When we have a detailed ethnography of officials' interaction with and mutual expectations from the gods we might well find a rather different view of the system: perhaps one stressing subordinates' unquestioning loyalty and incumbents' long-term occupancy of office.

But even if Chinese ritual did teach numerous important things about the political system, it also omitted a number of strikingly important things. In order to explain what was omitted, I must introduce data concerning a major lack of parallel in interactions with earthly and spiritual authorities. I asked a sample of Ch'inan villagers which human relationship most resembles that between man and god: student—teacher; child—parent; citizen—official; patient—doctor; upper—lower generations; or sister's son—mother's brother. Half expecting them to choose 'citizen–official', I was startled to find that the choice was almost invariably 'child–parent'. The following explanation is representative.

Parents teach their children to do good and the gods do the same. If you were sick your parents would want to help you. The gods are the same. As long as you do good deeds and respect them, they will exert their strength to the utmost to help. Parents will do likewise, if you are obedient and good. Neither gods nor parents want anything to do with delinquents and gangsters or useless, direction-less people.

Further questioning about relations between men and officials and men and gods led to shocked denials. I asked whether giving a local official a 'red envelope' in return for a favor was like making an offering to the gods. These are the kinds of answers I got:[8]

(1) The two things are entirely different. Giving red envelopes involves people mutually taking advantage of each other. Each party has a hold over the other: I can report the policeman and he can report me. Gods aren't the same at all. They will not help more as we give more. These are entirely different sorts of things.

(2) Red envelopes are not given for no reason. The point is to make the other party be good to us and not make trouble for us. So police act one way to people who give them red envelopes and another way to those who do not. But gods are not like that. It is not that the more things you give them the more they will help you. It is only necessary to do good deeds and burn three sticks of incense and they will be enormously happy. A god is a being with a very upright heart. He is fair and just, rewarding without favoritism.

(3) Offering things to the gods is just like taking a gift to one's host. A stranger won't necessarily help you no matter how nice a gift you bring, and a good friend will help even if you bring nothing at all.

Nor is making a pledge (*hi-guan*) like making a payment to an official. 'It is like begging one's parents for help: it shows how desperate our need is. When we are in need, gods and parents alike will really try to help us.'

What could be the explanation for these choices and denials? How can people dress out the gods and deal with them in an entirely bureaucratic fashion and then deny that their relationship to them is of the sort they have with living bureaucrats?

One possible explanation is that gods are considered to behave the way bureaucrats should ideally behave but seldom actually do behave. Just as parents ideally love their children impartially, benevolently, and attentively, and children respond with genuinely felt respect and care, so officials should behave and people respond. This view would reflect the line of Ch'ing writers on administration, who saw the local magistrate as the 'father and mother' of the common people, who were his 'newborn children' (Watt 1977: 362; 1972: 85–6). Despite these ideals, in actuality, officials are inaccessible, preoccupied, and corrupt, being influenced by bribes to subvert justice. In contrast, gods act toward citizens as officials ideally should (and as parents should toward children), impartially, benevolently, and attentively. If these views were held, it would explain the rejection of the idea that gods and officials are dealt with on the same basis.

Another explanation, which seems more accurate, is that although the conduct of some officials and some gods is similar, the internal organization of their two bureaucracies is different. This explanation depends on the following contrasting views being held of (1) the earthly bureaucracy on the one hand and (2) the spiritual bureaucracy on the other.

(1) High officials are in actual practice virtuous, upright, impartial, benevolent, and attentive. But they are blocked from access to ordinary people by a lower layer of rapacious underlings who accept bribes, carry on extortion, and bring every manner of legal entanglement or financial ruin on those who cannot avoid dealing with them.

There is considerable evidence that the underlings of officials did often behave in this manner during the Ch'ing dynasty on the mainland. Ch'ü details extensive forms of corruption practiced by magistrates' clerks, runners, and personal servants (1962: 49ff., 67ff., 88ff.). I know of little direct evidence that local people regarded this corruption as confined to the magistrates' underlings. But the experiences of R.F. Johnston, a British magistrate in Weihaiwei at the turn of the century, speaks indirectly to the question. When he altered the system of access to the court by abolishing the petition-writers who could be bribed or could extort, allowing the illiterate to present their cases orally, the local people deluged him with cases (1910: 103–4).[9] Evidently, once people discovered 'the ease with which the magistrate could be directly approached by the poorest litigant' and therefore the ease with which they could get direct access to the court's authority, they hastened to make use of it (p. 114).

In Taiwan people often speak of the local police and even petty officials accepting payment for favors, though no such elaborate system of corruption as in the Ch'ing seems to exist. From San-hsia there is direct evidence that people regard this sort of misdemeanor as usually limited to the lower levels of the bureaucracy. After an extensive scandal in the San-hsia township government, in which numerous officials lost their positions on charges of corruption, people explained it thus: 'The higher officials didn't know all this corruption was going on. When it was called to their attention, they cleared it out.' In the world of men, then, high officials (how high is left vague) are upright, but access to them is blocked by corrupt subordinates.

To say that access to high officials is blocked by subordinates is not necessarily to say that one cannot get access to them at all, but only that one normally has to proceed *through* subordinates. In the Ch'ing as in present day Taiwan, underlings (clerks, runners, secretaries) of the lowest official had to be dealt with before the official himself could be reached, and legal appeals normally moved from lower courts to higher ones (Ch'ü 1962: 120). Persons who, in desperation, attempted to break normal procedures by appealing directly to the highest official were sometimes subject to punishment (Bodde and Morris 1967: 466).[10]

(2) In the world of spirits, upright gods may have corrupt underlings, but men have direct, unimpeded access to the highest gods. The Taiwan data have already shown us that most high gods are regarded as virtuous, upright personages unsusceptible to bribery. As we have also seen in earlier chapters, ghostly subordinates of the gods and low-level gods like *Tho-te-kong* do accept or demand payment for favors granted. So far all seems parallel to the world of men. But there the similarity ends. Access to higher gods is *not* necessarily through the intermediation of underlings or low deities like *Tho-te-kong*. Although people sometimes do proceed through the mediation of a low god, they need not. Great favors and urgent help can be asked directly of *Thi:-kong*, the highest god. One can pray, divine, make offerings and deferential gestures directly to the object of one's attention.[11] Of course, the message might or might not get through. (Sometimes the gods are said to be too busy to be present in a particular image.) But messages are never, to my knowledge, held up because they have been waylaid by a subordinate spirit. The unimpeded character of access to higher gods is expressed also in the way offerings are made. Meat — raw and cooked — is sometimes offered to *Co-su-kong*. Informants said that he would accept the meat and (because he is a vegetarian) pass it on to his subordinates and soldiers. The sequence is petitioner — god — underling; in earthly bureaucracies it is petitioner — underling — official. Again, offerings are always made in temporal sequence to the highest god (*Thi:-kong*) first, then to other gods ranking below him, and then, depending on the occasion, to ghosts and gods' subordinates. This is partly a matter of respect, as when one serves the highest ranking guest first, but it is also a matter of access directly to the source of legitimate power.

The puzzle over the responses to my question would then be resolved this way: high officials *and* high gods are impartial, benevolent and attentive. So offerings to the high gods are not payments but tokens of respect given to perpetuate a valued relationship like that between parents and children. In contrast, low gods and ghosts, like low officials and their underlings, are open to the influence of special gifts, and care is taken to see they get them. The mistake in my questions was the implication that *all* gods are like the pragmatic low-level officials people ordinarily have to deal with. People find comparisons between high gods and high officials on the one hand, and low gods and low officials on the other, unobjectionable.

At this point we can see that in certain respects the structure of the earthly and spiritual bureaucracies is similar. But with regard to the kind of access people have to the highest powers, the two bureaucracies differ strikingly.[12] I would suggest this difference between the two worlds may represent an effort to hypothesize, and partly bring into actual effect, a solution to a problem people feel deeply. Here I am drawing on insights from analyses of other societies in which rituals seem to represent efforts to deal with (even if only by expressing) irresolvable or at least bothersome dilemmas.[13]

The problem in the Chinese case is how to get access to the upright and legitimate authority of high officials when they are shielded by corrupt underlings or are available only through subordinate and less upright officials. The answer in the spiritual context is that high gods are not so shielded: access to them is relatively open and unimpeded, either by corrupt underlings or by lower-order gods. This might be taken as the hypothetical statement: 'If the earthly bureaucracy were organized as the spiritual bureaucracy is, the problem of access to legitimate authority would be solved.' But the spiritual world does not represent only a hypothetical solution to a problem, it puts a solution into effect: high, powerful gods are thought to act on people's behalf, curing illness, bringing harmony, sons, or wealth.

To return to our hypothesis that people learned about the political system from the ritual system, the disanalogy we have been discussing might lead us to the conclusion that rituals involving gods would have conveyed seriously *wrong* information about the political system. Other disanalogies, of which there may be many, might lead to the same difficulty. One response to this is to suggest that whereas some aspects of the religious system may have taught facts about the political system in a straightforward way, others, in complementary fashion, may have represented solutions to problems (such as the ones I outlined just above) perceived to exist in the political system. Another possibility is that the ritual system with its disanalogies taught a particular practical way of dealing with the political system: that one should get as close to legitimate authority as possible, by skipping intermediate stages in the bureaucracy if necessary.

Such a strategy would contravene the normal procedure in Ch'ing times by which suits were adjudicated first in district magistrates' courts and then proceeded up through higher courts as necessary in fixed order (Bodde and Morris 1967: 117–18). There were penalties against taking a suit to a higher authority before passing through the district magistrate, penalties that were posted, along with the law, over the gate of the district administration office (Watt 1973: 213, 305). Many magistrates posted signs reading, '*Yüeh-sung* (to bypass the proper authorities and submit a complaint to the superior yamen) is punishable with fifty strokes' (Ku Yen-wu in Ch'ü 1962: 272 n1). But it was possible to circumvent the usual procedure. A private individual could appeal to a higher court, lodging an accusation or protesting a decision if his case was refused or handled incorrectly by the lower court (Bodde and Morris 1967: 118).[14]

Appeals such as this were dangerous, because the person making the appeal was himself subject to punishment if he failed to utilize all legal procedures at lower levels or if his accusations were judged untrue (Bodde and Morris 1967: 118). But they may have been regarded as worth the risk if the matter was serious enough and no other tactic available. In fact, if a citizen believed his case had been adjudicated improperly at one level of the bureaucracy, his only hope of redress would be through direct appeal to a higher level. Appeal to the official believed to be at fault would be doomed to failure, because he would very likely try to prevent a complaint about how he handled a case from reaching his superiors. Otherwise he might be penalized for misconduct, and the penalties were not trivial. Depending on the seriousness of his mistake, they ranged from forfeiture of salary or dismissal, to penal servitude, banishment, or death (Ch'ü 1962: 128–9).

The situation in post-1945 Taiwan is structurally similar, with official and legal matters normally being handled by local (township) authorities first, proceeding to higher (county) levels if necessary. In Taiwan, as in Ch'ing China, appeals directly to higher authorities can be made (Ku 1966: 100). It is possible that the strategy we have been discussing is even more useful in Taiwan. There is some indication that as landlords and lineage leaders – who traditionally mediated conflict before it reached the courts – decline in importance, people are more willing to submit to courts for arbitration (Gallin 1966: 273). The strategy of going to the top would be more relevant in dealing with legal authorities than in dealing with local mediators.

We have no comparative figures on the amount of litigation in Ch'ing China and Taiwan, let alone on how often appeals were made directly to high authorities, but in one Taiwan case we have already discussed – the Ongs' struggle to have a retaining wall built – the plaintiffs went directly to county officials, bypassing local township officials. As for the Ch'ing, the case described above by Hsiao (pp. 17–18) gives us one example, and the *Peking Gazette* contains many references to appeals made directly to the capital, in cases where bribery or the 'machinations of extortionate underlings' had resulted in a miscarriage of justice (2 Nov. 1878: 216; 6 Oct. 1882: 158; 16 Oct. 1882: 165). In other cases, local notables who had the ear of the magistrate misrepresented the facts, and the plaintiff appealed over the heads of all local personnel. A native of Chekiang complained that,

the head of their family having directed his cousin, Tung Hui-lan, to watch the crops at night, Tung Pu-yün and other members of the clan, grudging the watcher's fees, assembled and slew Tung Hui-lan and three other relations of the apellants. On the case coming before the Magistrate, the head of the clan and the constable of the village deponed that the deceased were of bad character and had excited general indignation by trying to extort those fees. On this the case was dismissed; and, as appeals to the Prefect, Judge, Intendant, and Governor have all been referred back to the magistrate, the apellant, his father having died of disappointment, has come to the capital to make his complaint (17 Oct. 1882: 166).

Summarizing the frustration of high level officials who were seemingly inundated by appeals, a case of 1870 declared: 'If the governors-general and governors would really handle cases conscientiously and straightforwardly, lawsuits would naturally diminish and there would be nothing like the number of accusations which in recent years have come to Peking from the provinces' (Bodde and Morris 1967: 466).

But it need not be argued that these appeals were statistically common.[15] It is enough to suggest that seeking direct access to high authority was highlighted by the ritual system as a possible strategy in appropriate circumstances. To say that the ritual system highlighted certain aspects of the political system is only to suggest that this metaphor directed attention in certain directions. In ordinary life we often deliberately use metaphors and analogies for this sort of purpose. Ryle comments, 'the golf-professional who tells me to think of my driver not as a sledge-hammer but as a rope with a weight on the end, expects me to cease to bang at the ball and to begin to sweep smoothly through the ball (1958: 140–1).

The strategy — going to the top — that seems to be thrown into relief by the ritual system fits with our overall understanding of Ch'ing administration. Recent studies have shown that although in some contexts local gentry (elite who were residing in their home territory and not holding office) acted as protectors of local people, in other contexts they allied themselves with local officials and yamen personnel for the purpose of furthering their own position — financial and social — at the expense of the local masses. As Watt describes it, gentry 'obtained preferential treatment in tax collection and support in litigation against commoners. Yamen personnel drummed up lucrative business for the gentry by delaying the processing of suits, which forced rural litigants to put up in town at hostels owned by gentry. Officials directed litigants to notaries, many of whom were down-at-heel gentry scholars' (1977: 363). In these contexts, it was not so much gentry as brokers and protectors of the local masses set against the yamen and its personnel, as it was gentry in collusion with local officials set against the local masses.

To the extent this was true, what recourse did the local masses have? Among other things, they could attempt to reach a level of the administration far enough away from local political involvement to act impartially, and this is precisely the strategy the ritual system seems to accentuate. The masses who were without social and economic power 'stood in a weaker relationship to the local yamen than to the central state' (Watt 1977: 384).

Other ways in which the ritual and political systems were not parallel must be put down to a fact I have already mentioned: the ritual we have been discussing reflects the vantage point of those in the society who were without much aspiration or hope of becoming holders of official power.[16] As we have seen, the source of a god's power, being *lieng*, is popular allegiance and confidence. In the notion of *lieng*, there is no parallel to the notions (common among aspiring elites) that entry into the national political arena necessitates a strong economic base in land and mercantile activities and diversification of economy in one's own kin group, such that some would run businesses and some study for civil exams (Lin 1948). Information about these important strategies would doubtless

have been useful for politically upward aspirants; however, for a group not con-
templating political activity, it might be far more compelling (and useful) to
dwell on the source of political authority in the allegiance of the masses, and its
moveable nature.

One might also argue for another lack of parallel. Since gods are almost
always seen as bureaucrats legitimized by office, the ritual system might ignore
one of the realities of local political power: local elite acting as informal leaders
of factions. People support one faction rather than another because they believe
they stand to gain particular social, political, or financial advantages: they are
often bound to particular leaders by a personal tie of a transient sort, based on
calculated self-interest; factional leaders and their constituents do not get the
sort of permanent rights and duties that go along with the incumbent of an
office and those under his authority.

We know that factions are the basis of much local political activity in Taiwan
and we may suspect they operated in the Ch'ing as well (Crissman 1981: 104–
16). If so, would not the gods, as office-holding bureaucrats, produce a picture that is wholly out of line with the way local politics actually operate? I
suspect not. Factions often operate only periodically, in election years in Taiwan
(Crissman 1981: 115–16), and the attention people pay to various factions is
not unlike the attention they pay to one god or another: both can be periodic
and changeable and both are dependent on people's estimates of how well
various superiors can fulfill their needs. And after the masses have demonstrated
decisive support for a candidate taking office, all the bureaucratic trappings of
the system become relevant, although factional alignments can also continue.
The fit between the two systems in this case reaches down to the organizational
level: cults focused on gods are sometimes the basis of political factions (Seaman
1974: 119–36).

The select nature of the metaphor Chinese religion presents of Chinese
politics allows us to reconsider the significance of the elaborate analogies
between social systems and religious systems that have been described since
Durkheim and his predecessors. In any case where there are analogies between
the religious sphere and some other sphere of ordinary life, we might ask whether
a teaching and learning 'game' is involved. *What* is learned need not relate only
to political matters, as it does in the case of Chinese gods. Even within the
Chinese context, if one looked at other kinds of ritual such as ancestor worship,
one would see themes related to interpersonal transaction (the nature of mutual
obligation and its limits) being dealt with, themes that relate more to kinsmen
and neighbors than to political authorities. In other societies, there is every
reason to expect very diverse material will be dealt with. Eventually we might be
able to understand in a systematic, comparative way why much of Chinese ritual
teaches about the nature of politics whereas ritual in other societies relates to
other themes. Surely the relative size, strength, endurance, and centralization of
the Chinese political system provides part of the answer. In at least one other

society with a powerful central state, contemporary Spain, there are also important parallels between the structure of earthly and spiritual powers and the strategies used to deal with them (Christian 1972: 173–4).

In a limited way, work that has already been done suggests some systematic comparisons. Bloch suggests that societies such as the Merina with 'traditional authority' are characterized by formalization in the political and ritual sphere. Among the Merina, formalized communication by elders in ritual contexts makes them virtual embodiments of the ancestors and thus of traditional authority (1974: 78). In societies that lack traditional authority, most formalization in ritual is absent (1975: 14). But it might be possible to relate the form of ritual even more precisely to the form of political authority. There are many different sorts of traditional authority, and we might expect formalization to take as many different forms. It is surely no accident that formalization in Chinese ritual occurs not just in interactions with the ancestors as the representatives of traditional kinship morality, but also in interactions with spiritual bureaucrats like those who exercised state control. The Merina restricted-ritual catechism in which elders control others by limiting their responses is the equivalent, in the Chinese case, of form-letters sent between bureaucrat and citizen. But in both cases interaction with spirits puts into play the same principles of control that operate in the political order: in the working of the religious system one *sees* the working of the political system.

To summarize the argument of Chapters 6 and 7, we can see that any simple claim that Chinese ritual and religion served the ends of those with political authority must be misleading unless it admits the possibility that the religion also served some useful purpose for those with no political authority. Unfortunately, all the claims I have discussed for what function the ritual and religion had are far from proven: for the moment they must remain simply hypotheses. But at least one point has become clear: even if Chinese ritual and religion did serve the ends of political authorities in some ways, as I allow in Chapter 6, it could *still* have served the ends of the powerless in other ways.

Let me end by addressing a problem specifically related to contemporary China and Taiwan. Observers have often wondered why ritual activities directed to gods in the form of Ch'ing bureaucrats continue and even flourish in Taiwan today despite the end of the Ch'ing dynasty and the introduction of substantial economic changes. These rituals have been described as anachronistic, as if they continued to exist through a kind of inertia. One could argue that the rituals continue because they continue to serve important social functions, allowing people to mark and express community solidarity, for example. This would account for the existence of *some* form of ritual but not for the particular form that in fact exists. If all that rituals do is to mark local communities, any number of forms would do as well.

Another explanation would begin by noting that despite changes in the economic structure of the society as a result of land reform, among other things, the structural features of the central government have remained largely the same as in Ch'ing times. The Kuomintang is centralized, bureaucratic, and hierarchical just as the Ch'ing state was, and the list of sociological features discussed above would largely apply to it as well. If rituals in Taiwan continue to 'talk about' politics, and in particular about structural features of the political system, then it should be no surprise that far-reaching changes have not been observed in the ritual system. Change of personnel there has been – photographs of Chiang Kai Shek can now be seen on temple altars – but this is merely an extension of an old feature of the system: the replacement of old gods by new ones who have proven their efficacy.

Consider briefly the situation in the People's Republic in recent years. In an early speech, Mao said that the peasants would abandon their gods when they saw that their problems could be solved in other ways:

The gods? Worship them by all means. But if you had only Lord Kuan and the Goddess of Mercy and no peasant association, could you have overthrown the local tyrants and evil gentry? The gods and goddesses are indeed miserable objects. You have worshipped them for centuries, and they have not overthrown a single one of the local tyrants or evil gentry for you! Now you want to have your rent reduced. Let me ask, how will you go about it? Will you believe in the gods or in the peasant association?

My words made the peasants roar with laughter (1965: I, 47).

Collectivization may have changed the economic face of society and even made it less necessary to seek help from the gods. But we have seen that Chinese ritual directed to the gods not only seemed to give people economic help, it also threw the nature of power and authority into relief. This may help us understand why, despite the end of most traditional ritual activities, new ones with explicitly political content were quick to arise.

In the early 1940s in the Border Region of north China, drought, famine, and war drove people, in part responding to ideas introduced by the Communist 8th Route Army, to overthrow their gods:

Meeting little opposition, the more active village officials sprang into the temples, tore the idols from their foundations and broke their heads off with stones. Their fantastic forms and features, conveying a symbolic meaning which had long been forgotten by most and was entirely lost on the younger men, seemed in their eyes only the remnants of a superstition that must die. With unaccustomed energy they rolled the broken idols out of the temples into the streets, amid the misgivings of the village elders. They then consummated the whole by smearing the gods with paint and by smashing them in front of the assembled farmers (Belden 1949: 63).

Even if people had forcibly removed the old spiritual officials from their positions, they were no less willing to allow a new official a chance:

Some villagers reached the conclusion that it was better to depend on themselves and Mao Tze-tung than on a god. They did not at this time replace their deities with Mao, but when the famine was finally broken and good times returned, not a few peasant families put little pictures of Mao in the tiny household shrines where they had formerly kept clay images (p. 63).

In the late 1960s factory workers set up 'Treasured Book Platforms', special tables where the four volumes of Mao's selected works were displayed and behind which a portrait of Mao hung. It was customary to 'seek guidance' there in the morning and to 'report' at night (MacInnis 1972: 338). Peasant households today commonly have a high table (sometimes the old altar they formerly used for ancestral tablets and gods' images) arranged in the usual place of honor opposite the main door with photographs of various political figures hung above it.[17]

Unfortunately, these glimpses of new political rituals in the People's Republic are not complete enough to suggest whether their form has changed so that they could convey strategic information about dealing with new political structures. We must be satisfied with seeing that people continue to represent the content of the political world to themselves, leaving open the question whether in the People's Republic, as in Taiwan and late Imperial China, religion and ritual mystified the nature of power in some ways but clarified it in others.

Conclusions and further questions

With regard to the relation between politics and ritual, China may well be an extreme case whose virtue is that it shows us what is true elsewhere, in varying and often lesser degrees. Perhaps because of the enormous extent of the territory governed by the Chinese state, or the length of time (over 2,000 years) it has maintained centralized control, the notion of power in the imagination of ordinary citizens is of only one sort in both the 'secular' and the 'religious' realm: the sort exercised by holders of hierarchical, bureaucratic offices. It is for this reason that the worlds of men and of spirits appear to be flat or uniform, with little to distinguish the kinds of effect on the world or other persons that operate in each. In a society with such tremendous depth between a peasant at the bottom and the emperor at the top, *that* distance must have seemed far more awesome than the distance between humans and spirits. From the perspective of peasants, the incorporeal earth-god must have seemed much more a part of the same social universe than the corporeal, but enormously far removed, emperor. And, for that matter, peasants would have had far more interactions with local spirits than with distant officials.

But if this characterization of the notion of power in China is generally true, its usefulness has scarcely begun to be tapped. What we need now are systematic studies within the Chinese political realm to see how placement in class, space, time, or political context causes the relation between political control and ritual to vary. For example, are communities less under the impress of state control (because of economic or geographic isolation, among other things) less caught up in a single idea of power as essentially political?[1] During times in which state control faltered (the decline of a dynasty or the struggle for one's establishment) was the legitimacy of spiritual officials thrown into question?[2] Do minority ritual traditions (heterodox sects, or Buddhism, for example) see the world with a politically more skeptical eye, and if so, what does their ritual have to say about the political system?[3] How, as I have wondered several times in the course of this monograph, did ritual as performed and interpreted by political elites differ from that of peasants?

In discussing Chinese ritual and politics, I have stressed at length that the

109

mechanisms of control in the world of spirits and of men are the same, and that, therefore, our vocabulary describing the efficacy of action should be the same for both. However, it is well to remember, as I cautioned along the way, that the *organization* of the two worlds can be quite different. There are differences between the way the world of human officials is organized and the way the world of the gods is organized in China, such as the extent of direct access to legitimate authority. It would be useful to have a comparative perspective on this issue and, in addition, of the various uses that I suggest these differences might serve, to have more direct evidence about which — if any — they actually do serve. Should they be described as efforts to solve bothersome dilemmas? Ways of teaching practical strategies? Or simply ways in which the limited perspective of peasants puts its mark on the world of spirits?

Several benefits have come out of my treatment of the formal properties of Chinese ritual. Seeing that interpersonal divination often involves restricted codes whereas non-interpersonal divination does not, has allowed us to separate two kinds of divination — systems of knowledge and systems of access to the gods' knowledge — and to suggest that open and closed forms of divination relate differently to political authority. Realizing that the restricted codes often found in ritual inherently involve artificial simplification has given us a way of understanding Chinese ritual as a teaching device and consequently a way of attaining a more balanced view of the claim that religion and ritual mystify their adherents and conceal the true nature of political power from them. The way is now cleared for us to ask under what conditions Chinese ritual talks or teaches about politics and why it conceals what it conceals, and reveals what it reveals.

Notes

Introduction

1 For romanizing Hokkien words and names I follow the system outlined in Bodman 1955, except that tone-marks have been omitted. All persons involved in my fieldwork have been given pseudonyms. I have romanized names of places and administrative units in Mandarin, using standard post-office spelling for well-known places and the Wade-Giles system for the rest. Some well-known terms are also given in their Mandarin forms. Mandarin and Hokkien spellings are distinguished in the Character list.

1. Interpersonal versus non-interpersonal transaction

1 It would take me too far afield to discuss here, but the Chinese category that is something like our category of person is closely tied up with possession of a soul (*lieng-hun*). All adult humans have souls, though they can get separated from the body, causing illness or insanity. Children before birth and under the age of four have souls that are relatively loosely attached to their bodies. Some animals (pigs and water-buffaloes) have souls, spirits (ancestors, gods, and ghosts) *are* souls, lacking bodies altogether. (See Harrell 1979.)
2 See also Finnegan 1969, Ray 1973, and Skorupski (1976: 130–4).
3 As one thoughtful man told me, 'the gods' help is "turning bad luck into good": they can reduce the impact of a very bad circumstance, or remove a minor difficulty entirely, but they are not always entirely able to control things'.

2. Written bureaucratic communication

1 See also Watt (1977: 377). The question why written documents played such a large role in the government would be too large to discuss here, but it seems obvious that, given the size and complexity of the bureaucracy and its geographical extent, communication could not easily be achieved any other way. (See Goody 1968 and 1977 for general discussions of literacy.) Another factor, less often appreciated, is that a written document allows a message to be effectively separated from the person who delivers it. Baker describes one of the difficulties with verbal communications in early twentieth-century business firms in China: 'A Chinese

executive who wishes to put an order into effect, calls his assistant, the assistant calls a clerk, the clerk calls a servant, the servant tells the coolie and the coolie goes to the department that is to receive the order; there he tells the doorman, the doorman tells a servant, the servant tells the most inferior clerk and finally the message is "relayed" up to the official addressed. By this time a most preemptory order would have become a most humble request' (1928: 394). In contrast, a written message can be delivered by a messenger with gestures and words appropriate to his status and yet still retain the impact originally intended by the author when read.

2   See Ahern (1973: 32—4) for a lengthier account of this dispute.

3   Lu gives models of these thank-you notes: one for 'accepting everything', one for 'accepting a part', one for 'accepting a second time', and one for 'not accepting any' (1864: 30—1).

4   A document similar in function is prepared when elaborate paper houses and furnishings are burned for the dead in the underworld. A slip of paper is prepared stating the dimensions of the house and burned to transfer it to the underworld. I was told: 'It is as if we were selling it to the deceased.'

5   McCreery (1973: 167) gives an example of a charm for 'harmonious co-operation' which addresses commands directly to the people concerned, demanding 'that their hearts and mouths and their words and deeds should be day and night harmonious'.

6   See Saso (1978: 144—50) for numerous other examples of Taoist spells.

7   Des Rotours discusses the meaning of the term *fu* (the Mandarin pronunciation of *hu*) among officials in the T'ang and subsequent dynasties. In most cases it was not an order *per se*, but an object divided into two parts. Half could be given to someone delegated to carry out a mission, deliver, or execute an order, and half kept by the authorities who originated the mission or order. The purpose was to authenticate the order or mission: if the two halves of the *fu* fit together, the source of the half accompanying the emissary could not be in doubt (1952: 117, 125—7).

8   To avoid too detailed a discussion, I have omitted consideration of how these charms were written. De Groot analyzes some of the principles of writing them (1969: VI, 1306) as do Ch'en (1942) and Doré (1965—7: III). There is one example in Eitel (1867: 164) and many in Doré (1965—7: I—II) and Li (1800).

3. Etiquette and control

1   Similarly, Sherry Ortner suggests that an invitation among Sherpa 'takes the form of a disguised command which it is virtually impossible to disobey' and invitations to the gods 'do not ask but actually conjure the gods into coming' (1975: 147).

2   To avoid an excess of ethnographic detail, I have omitted consideration of gestures and body posture as ways of communicating deference or superiority. In large part, the same messages communicated verbally can be communicated gesturally, and, as with verbal communication, there is an elaborate parallel between gestures used among men and gestures used between men and spirits.

3   Saso discusses the jealously guarded Taoist ritual names for certain spirits (1978: 156—60).

4   In 1969 NT$40 = US$1.

112

5   Just as the likelihood of a gift being accepted varies with the status of the recipient, so does the form of the gift. Officials and police are given presents commensurate with their status and so are gods and other spirits. It has been shown more than once that the form of food (cooked or uncooked, vegetable or meat, whole or cut up, seasoned or not) as well as the kind of ritual money and number of sticks of incense offered are determined by the rank of gods, ancestors, and ghosts relative to man's position in the scheme of things or to the position of the particular person making the offering (Ahern 1973: 167–70; Feuchtwang 1974a; Harrell 1974; Hou 1975; Wolf 1974a: 178–82).

4. Divination

1   There are various other ways to *thiu-chiam*. In one temple in San-hsia the slips are obtained from a coin-operated machine. The machine shortens the procedure, combining the 'random' choice of a bamboo lot and the matching of the lot to the proper *chiam*. Although people said the god still controlled which slip came out of the machine, they felt this method was less 'accurate' than the usual one. Another alternative is to use a do-it-yourself handbook, tossing a pair of coins in place of the *pue* (*Kuan-sheng-ti-chün* 1971).
2   See Doolittle (1966: II, 333–4); Gray (1878: II, 6) for descriptions of similar kinds of divination.
3   See Doolittle (1966: II, 336–7) for an account of a similar practitioner.
4   See Jordan (1972: 66ff.); Elliott (1955: 140–5); Doolittle (1966: II,110ff.).
5   This is not necessarily the case. Jordan reports a case in which a *tang-ki*'s speech was so garbled that writing divination was used to get a clarification (1972: 77).
6   In this sort of divination, it is natural for people to make attempts to confirm that the message in fact comes from the desired source. As Jordan describes it: 'Various devices are tried in order to separate godly possession from ghostly possession. Initiations of *tâng-ki* accordingly include exorcism and trial by miracles. Thus when Guo Ching-shoei was initiated as medium of the Great Saint in 1968 he was required to splash boiling oil on his face with his bare hands. He suffered no harm because he was protected by his god; a demonic presence would not have been able to stand by him in this way, but would have fled in terror, leaving Ching-shoei to be burned.

There are such things as false *tâng-ki*, by which I mean *tâng-ki* who are possessed by no presence at all, be it divine or diabolic. These men merely imitate the behavior of possessed *tâng-ki* to defraud the public by charging for the 'services' they render. They are known as 'divine rascals'. In general they are urban, because it is more usual for urban *tâng-ki* to accept cash for their trance performances' (1972: 74). Authenticity of the writing oracle is proved if the bearers of the chair are illiterate and thus could not be producing the characters themselves (Jordan 1972: 66).
7   The geomancer may be perceived as giving information *about* other beings: ordinary people sometimes regard the 'dragon-force' of the geomancer's vocabulary as a dragon-being. But the geomancer would only be telling them where the dragon was located or how strong it was on the basis of his observations or calculations. The dragon would not have sent messages to him.

113

8   Moore (1957) has suggested that the randomizing device may have adaptive functions. In the case of the Naskapi it may prevent over-hunting by directing hunters in random directions.

9   Several attempts have been made to specify the characteristics of this kind of truncated language. Basil Bernstein uses the term to refer to language in which 'the verbal component of the message, given the social context, is highly predictable' (1964: 58). This is because 'the range of alternatives, syntactic alternatives, is considerably reduced' compared to the alternatives available in ordinary, spoken language (p. 57). He is concerned with a wide range of types including restricted codes in which there is lexicon prediction and those in which there is syntactic prediction. The most restricted type involving lexicon prediction, the case of most interest here, is a code in which the organization and selection of all signals is bound by 'rigid and extensive prescriptions'. There are few options open to the individual who is a 'cultural agent' (p. 58). In less restricted codes with lexicon prediction, non-verbal aspects of communication (gestures, expression) are less predictable.

     Maurice Bloch describes 'formalized speech acts' in which loudness patterns are fixed, choice of intonation and vocabulary is limited, some syntactic forms are excluded, the sequence of speech acts is fixed, illustrations come from certain limited sources, and stylistic rules are consciously applied (1974: 60). Roy Rappaport talks of the contrast between 'continuous analogic or *more-or-less* information' in ordinary life and the simpler '*yes–no* statement of ritual occurrence' (1971: 27); and D.K. Lewis describes a 'verbal signalling language' in which there is a finite set of sentences reserved for use in some particular activity in which the users have little free choice (Lewis 1969: 160ff.). There is clearly some overlap in these descriptions: the analysts are all after a kind of linguistic activity in which choice of the speaker is more restricted, whether lexically, syntactically, or stylistically, than it is in other linguistic activities. What is said is therefore more predictable than in other forms of linguistic activity.

10   Because these topics are quite general, they usually retain their usefulness over time. In some cases, however, anachronisms appear: one set of topics includes 'silkworms', which may have been relevant when the slips originated but certainly is not today. (See Ch. 7, note 5.) This sort of anachronism is of course created by the 'frozen' shape of the code: once agreements are reached with distant parties, they are not easily adjusted. Maurice Bloch's comments on the 'arthritic' nature of ritual language are very relevant here (1975: 19).

11   See Doré (1965–7: IV, 321–6) and Chao 1946 for descriptions of the relevant categories.

12   In this Chapter I have limited the discussion to divination's formal features, deflecting attention from the more usual anthropological concern with its social or psychological functions. Some of these will be discussed in Chapters 6 and 7; I will briefly comment on some others below.

     Bohannan has suggested that Tiv divination establishes 'a sort of quasi-communication between the diviner and his oracles, which in fact *hides* the sources of actual communication among the petitioners of the oracle' (1975: 151). 'The oracle itself is primarily a distracting device that allows the principals to construct an explanation that can be handled' (p. 166). The real communication he refers to is, of course, the process by which the diviner, client, and bystanders analyze their own social situations, revealing conflict and assigning blame. I would only add that, as we have seen, it is in the nature of any restricted code to require elaborate interpretation because of the impossibility of including very many specific messages. Where the gods possess a *tang-ki* and speak as freely as they wish, more or less interpretation is required by the client, depending on how much the *tang-ki* says. In either case, it is in the process of making general prognostications apply to a particular case or attempting to make a god's elliptical remarks relevant that real moral and sociological analysis often goes on.

It has often been held that this kind of analysis has an important function in relieving anxiety. Beattie puts it this way: 'Divination involves a vivid dramatic performance . . . [it has] a cathartic quality . . . [It is] a way of expressing, and so of relieving, some of the interpersonal stresses and strains which are inseparable from life in a small-scale community' (1964: 61). Others have argued in various ways that the outcome of a divinatory session also relieves anxiety by reducing indecision. 'On the personal side, the function of divination in imparting confidence, offering consolation, and giving guidance during a crisis is quite apparent' (Yang 1961: 261–2).

'The hypothesis would seem to be highly plausible that the practice of divinatory rituals has the effects of: reducing the duration of individual indecision; accomplishing a more rapid consensus within a group, with minimal offense to the members; and inspiring the persons who must execute the decision with sufficient confidence to permit them to mobilize their full skills and energies, unimpeded by anxiety, fear, or doubts about having made the best choice among the alternatives available' (Wallace 1966: 173). (See also Vogt (1952: 185) and Csikszentmihalyi and Bennett (1971: 49) for similar views.)

I would not want to question that these descriptions of divinatory sessions are sometimes accurate. But, at the same time, it must be added that divination can also create anxiety. I was struck by the response a young woman made to my invitation to go along to a temple to *thiu-chiam*. She said she had done so several times recently and the slips she had drawn had been so bad she had become quite depressed. She declined the invitation in order to avoid another upsetting experience. Williams' description is not far from accurate: 'The countenances of worshippers as they leave the shrines, some beaming with hope and resolution to succeed, and others, notwithstanding their repeated knockings and divinings, going away with vexation and gloom written on their faces at the obduracy of the gods and sadness of their prospects, offer a study not less melancholy than instructive' (1965: II, 260).

It is obvious from the way some oracle slips (*chiam*) are coded that some must be good and some bad. They are sometimes marked 'good' (*tieng-tieng*), 'bad' (*e-e*) or 'middling' (*tiong-pia:*) such that 25 per cent are good, 25 per cent bad and 50 per cent middling (Eberhard 1970: 193 and Allen 1872b: 507–21). As Kleinman notes, *chiam* interpreters may soften the worst oracles in various ways (1975: 35) but the fact remains that many people do not seek out an interpreter, but simply read the slip on their own. It is hard to see how the 'bad' oracle quoted above (p. 61) or the one below could be comforting to a person in a state of worried indecision: 'The great Huang-yu was a brave valiant man, but though he ruled over 10,000 miles of hill and river, of a sudden he lost it all, and of all his clan of 8,000 none remained. With what feelings think you did he return to Chiang-tung' (Allen 1872b: 507).

5. Open and closed practices

1 In addition to Searle's discussion of constitutive and regulative rules, this distinction draws on Friedrich Waismann's discussion of open texture in concepts (1965a), H.L.A. Hart's discussion of open texture in law (1961: 120—32), and John Rawls' discussion of rules (1955).

2 The distinction between open and closed practices differs from characterizations of *societies* as open or closed (Jarvie 1964: 115—16, 118ff.; Horton 1967). When the focus is on practices rather than whole societies, it is unlikely that any society would appear entirely closed or entirely open. Some portions would appear more closed than others. The distinction I am using is similar to one made by F.C. Bartlett in 1946 between 'hard' and 'soft' points in a culture (1946: 145).

3 Feuerwerker (1975: 57) suggests that the revolutionary character of the Taiping ideology was a rarity among Chinese nineteenth-century rebel groups.

6. Ritual and political authorities

1 Religious systems often bear very differently on women than they do on men. Christian describes how the religion of Spanish villagers is explicitly recognized to be a way of keeping women in line (1972: 177). In Ahern 1975 and Seaman 1981 this issue is discussed with regard to notions of pollution in China.

2 See *Peking Gazette* (1880: 10, 1881: 82) for other examples.

3 There were of course other motives for requesting canonization. Sometimes officials were bribed to do so (Hsiao 1960: 227). It is also possible that a posthumous honor to a former resident of an administrative area brought honor to the current administrator.

4 See Feuchtwang (1977: 592—6) for discussion of ways official religion was intended to exert ideological control.

5 Geisert (1977) describes the tension and conflict among Kuomintang members, non-Kuomintang local officials, and local citizens over the worship of local gods in Kiangsu Province, 1927—37.

6 It should be added that another reason the Taiwan government has begun forcibly to restrict the extent of *pai-pais* is that they absorb resources for local purposes that the government would like spent on its national priorities. See Ahern 1981.

7 The government also outlawed other forms of writing that involved assertion of authority. A Ch'ing government proclamation included a regulation against erecting placards in the path of a god's procession, 'declaring that such and such a place is the promenade or the abode of a certain god: . . . as for instance "The promenade of the eldest son Duke Wei-ling" or of General Ma, or of Tartar General Wen, . . . just as if a coolie's abode could be the abode of a noble' (Allen 1872c: 518).

8 Lewis 1971 has addressed this question in an extended analysis of spirit possession.

9　See Yang (1961: 261—2) for another oracle with a Confucian bent.

10　*Ch'ien* were also used as lots to randomize the assignment of civil appoint-
ments to various provinces (Huang 1893: I, chüan 1, pp. 3—4) and they
are used in Taiwan today to randomize the assignment of soldiers to their
posts.

11　*Ch'ien* are illustrated in the frontispiece of this book, in Smith (1970:
164) and in a posed photograph in Warner n.d. I am grateful to Sue
Naquin for these last references.

12　De Groot (1969: VI, 1271) says only insignificant, low gods will possess a
medium. Where this is true, the authority of a medium's pronouncement
might be diminished on this account. In Taiwan and elsewhere (Elliott
1955: 74—9) powerful, high gods regularly possess men.

13　See Yang (1961: 263) and Chesneaux (1971: 52—3) on the I-kuan Tao
sect. Chao (1942: 10—11) describes a twentieth-century secret society that
used spirit writing. On government suppression of spirit writing sects in
China and Taiwan, see Seaman (1974: 20—2).

7. Ritual as a learning game

1　Tambiah (1973: 213) obliquely suggests the possibility that ritual might
be like a teaching device.

2　See Seaman (1974: 96) on the image of a god as the physical representation of an office.

3　Seaman (1974: 65) shows how the hierarchy of the gods is expressed in
the location of their images in the temple. Feuchtwang points out an
important distinction between the kind of hierarchy recognized among the
temples of official religion and that recognized among the temples of
popular religion (1977: 590). In the former, temples were ranked according to administrative level. In the latter, a temple of a particularly powerful deity could have branch temples formed by the process known as
'division of incense' (*fen-hsiang*). Devotees who wished to form a new
temple founded it on a pot of incense taken from the old temple, quite
without regard to the administrative level of the new temple's location.
(See Schipper 1977: 652 on *fen-hsiang*.)

4　E. Goody has made the related point that greetings given to chiefs among
the Gonja are regarded as things of value: they are gifts of respect and
deference that communicate political support (1972: 61, 67).

5　The following chart shows the topics on divination slips for Kuan-yin in
Hong Kong (*Kuan-yin Ling-ch'ien* n.d.) compared to those on slips for
Co-su-kong in Ting-p'u in northern Taiwan.

Ting-p'u, Taiwan	Hong Kong
	Identical
hsin-jen (searching for a person)	hsin-jen
liu-chia (pregnancy)	liu-chia
ch'iu-ts'ai (seeking wealth)	ch'iu-ts'ai
chi-ping (sickness)	chi-ping
shih-wu (lost goods)	shih-wu
hun-yin (marriage)	hun-yin
	Similar
yun-t'u (journey)	hsing-jen (traveller)

Ting-p'u, Taiwan	Hong Kong
	Similar (cont.)
tz'u-sung (litigation)	kung-sung (litigation)
i-chu (moving)	i-ts'ung (moving)
	Unlike
tso-shih (carrying out affairs)	chia-chia (household)
ping-jen (sick person)	tzu-shen (oneself)
nien-chung (year end)	chiao-i (trade)
kung-ming (fame)	t'ien-ts'an (fields, silkworms)
ch'iu-yü (seek rain)	shan-fen (graves)
ch'u-hsing (affairs outside)	liu-ch'u (six domestic animals)
kuan-shih (official affair)	
ta-ming (fate)	
sui-chün (the year)	
lai-jen (person coming)	

6   A more straightforward example of standardized forms comes from a spirit writing cult in central Taiwan. Supplicants communicate with the gods via cult members, using 'printed forms which are filled out with the supplicants' [*sic*] name and age and his business with the gods' (Seaman 1974: 65).

7   See Howe 1977 on the didactic functions of political metaphors.

8   Many people made vague condemnations to the effect that other people sometimes try to manipulate the gods by making special offerings. They insisted these efforts would be doomed to failure.

9   Johnston also provided a locked letter-box for those who were afraid to submit suits in open court (1910: 114—15).

10   Some of those who petitioned Ch'ing emperors were successful in gaining a hearing. The K'ang-hsi emperor wrote about cases brought to him while he was on tour (Spence 1974: 43).

11   Access to the upright (*cieng*) gods in heaven is direct, but access to the bureaucracy of the underworld is, like the earthly bureaucracy, shielded by rapacious subordinates. *Tho-te-kong* must pay off gate-keepers, bridge-toll takers, and other spirits before they will allow the soul of the dead to pass.

12   In his fieldwork in Spanish villages, Christian found that the main types of transaction among humans are found in transactions with the divine (1972: 172). This is true in the Chinese case, but the most important point is that the way transactions are *used* differs in the two cases.

13   Geertz (1972) has recently adopted this approach, as has Ortner (1975).

14   See Bodde and Morris (1967: 352—4; 461—7) for cases involving such appeals.

15   In the Ming dynasty, direct appeals to the emperor were not uncommon. A private citizen could submit a memorial to the emperor himself, handing it in at any government office. In Szechwan Province alone, in a period of less than four years, more than 200 such appeals were made (Hucker 1966: 99).

16   For another example, the peasants' ritual system contained little elaboration of informal interrelations among gods (and, by analogy, among officials). It also did not elaborate means whereby higher officials double-checked information from below: for example, the system of 'palace

memorials' begun by the K'ang-hsi emperor whereby secret missives were sent to the emperor with information that might otherwise have been concealed (Wu 1970: 35).

17 Elisabeth Croll, personal communication. See also Chen (1973: 7); Welch 1970; and Whyte (1974: 155).

Conclusions and further questions

1 Skinner (1977) gives a cogent analysis of the kinds of differences that existed between economically and administratively central as opposed to peripheral areas in the Ch'ing.

2 See Li Wei-tsu (1948: 21—2, 24—5) for a case in which, during a time of political contention, gods were said to desert their images in favor of animal spirits.

3 See Myron Cohen's paper (1976), which is suggestive in this light. Robert Weller's work in Taiwan (1980) indicates that there are fundamental differences between local Buddhists' views of the spiritual world and those of lay villagers.

119

Bibliography

Ahern, Emily M. 1973. *The Cult of the Dead in a Chinese Village*. Stanford: Stanford University Press
    1975. 'The Power and Pollution of Chinese Women', pp. 193–214 in Margery Wolf and Roxane Witke, eds., *Women in Chinese Society*. Stanford: Stanford University Press
    1981. 'The Thai Ti Kong Festival', in Emily Martin Ahern and Hill Gates, eds., *The Anthropology of Taiwanese Society*. Stanford: Stanford University Press
Aijmer, Göran. 1968. 'Being Caught by a Fishnet: On Fengshui in Southeastern China', *Journal of the Royal Asiatic Society: Hong Kong Branch*, 8: 74–81
Allen, C.F.R., trans. 1872a. 'Twenty-eight Temple Oracles or Stanzas', pp. 504–7 in Rev. Justus Doolittle, ed., *A Vocabulary and Handbook of the Chinese Language*, vol. II. Foochow: Rozario, Marcal and Company
    trans. 1872b. 'Fifty-six Temple Oracles or Stanzas', pp. 507–12 in Rev. Justus Doolittle, ed., *A Vocabulary and Handbook of the Chinese Language*, vol. II. Foochow: Rozario, Marcal and Company
    trans. 1872c. 'Proclamation Against Idol Processions: Issued at Fuchow', pp. 516–18 in Rev. Justus Doolittle, ed., *A Vocabulary and Handbook of the Chinese Language*, vol. II. Foochow: Rozario, Marcal and Company
Austin, J.L. 1962. *How to Do Things with Words*. New York: Oxford University Press
Baker, John Earl. 1928. 'Why Chinese Business is not Business: Ways in which Confucian Etiquette Hinders the Industrialization of China', *Asia*, 28, 5: 390–7; 426–7
Balazs, Etienne. 1965. *Political Theory and Administrative Reality in Traditional China*. London: School of Oriental and African Studies
Bartlett, Sir F.C. 1946. 'Psychological Methods for the Study of Hard and Soft Features of Culture', *Africa*, 16: 145–55
Bascom, W.R. 1941. 'The Sanctions of Ifa Divination', *Journal of the Royal Anthropological Institute*, 71: 43–53
Bateson, Gregory. 1972. *Steps to an Ecology of Mind*. New York: Ballantine Books
Beattie, John. 1964. 'Divination in Bunyoro, Uganda', *Sociologus*, 14, 1: 44–61
Belden, Jack. 1949. *China Shakes the World*. New York: Monthly Review Press
Bernstein, Basil. 1964. 'Elaborated and Restricted Codes: Their Social Origins

120

and Some Consequences', *American Anthropologist* Special Publication, 66, 6; part 2: 55–69

Black, Max. 1962. *Models and Metaphors: Studies in Language and Philosophy.* Ithaca: Cornell University Press

Blau, Peter M. 1974. *On the Nature of Organizations.* New York: John Wiley and Sons

Bloch, Maurice. 1974. 'Symbols, Song, Dance and Features of Articulation: Is Religion an Extreme Form of Traditional Authority?' *European Journal of Sociology* 15: 55–81

   1975. 'Introduction', pp. 1–28 in *Political Language and Oratory in Traditional Society.* New York: Academic Press

Bodde, Derk and Clarence Morris. 1967. *Law in Imperial China: Exemplified by 190 Ch'ing Dynasty Cases (Translated from the Hsing-an hui-lan) with Historical, Social and Juridical Commentaries.* Cambridge, Mass.: Harvard University Press

Bodman, Nicholas C. 1955. *Spoken Amoy Hokkien.* Kuala Lumpur: Grenier and Son

Bohannan, P.J. 1975. 'Tiv Divination', pp. 149–66 in J.H.M. Beattie and R.G. Lienhardt, eds., *Studies in Social Anthropology: Essays in Memory of E.E. Evans-Pritchard by his Former Oxford Colleagues.* London: Oxford University Press

Bourdillon, M.F.C. 1978. 'Knowing the World or Hiding it: A Response to Maurice Bloch'. *Man,* 13, 4: 591–99.

Bredon, Juliet and Igor Mitrophanow. 1927. *The Moon Year.* Shanghai: Kelly and Walsh, Ltd

Chao Wei-pang. 1942. 'The Origin and Growth of the *Fu Chi*', *Folklore Studies,* 1: 9–27

   1946. 'The Chinese Science of Fate Calculation', *Folklore Studies* 5: 279–315.

Chen, Jack. 1973. *A Year in Upper Felicity: Life in a Chinese Village During the Cultural Revolution.* London: Harrap

Ch'en Hsiang-ch'un. 1942. 'Examples of Charms Against Epidemics with Short Explanations', *Folklore Studies,* 1: 37–54

Chesneaux, Jean. 1971. *Secret Societies in China in the Nineteenth and Twentieth Centuries.* Trans. Gillian Nettle. London: Heinemann Educational Books

Christian, William Armistead. 1972. *Person and God in a Spanish Valley.* New York: Academic Press

Ch'ü, T'ung-tsu. 1962. *Local Government in China under the Ch'ing.* Cambridge, Mass.: Harvard University Press

Cohen, Myron L. 1976. 'Taiwanese Society and Anthropological Perspectives on Chinese Religion', paper prepared for the Conference on Anthropology in Taiwan

Committee of the Royal Anthropological Institute of Great Britain and Ireland, A. 1951. *Notes and Queries on Anthropology.* Sixth edn

Cormack, Mrs J.G. 1922. *Chinese Birthday, Wedding, Funeral, and other Customs.* Peking: China Booksellers, Ltd

Couchoud, Paul Louis, ed. 1928. *Mythologie asiatique illustrée.* Paris

Crissman, Lawrence W. 1981. 'The Structure of Local and Regional Systems', in Emily Martin Ahern and Hill Gates, eds., *The Anthropology of Taiwanese Society.* Stanford: Stanford University Press

Bibliography

Csikszentmihalyi, Mihaly and Stith Bennett. 1971. 'An Exploratory Model of Play', *American Anthropologist*, 73: 45–58

Cullen, J.M. 1972. 'Some Principles of Animal Communication', pp. 101–25 in R.A. Hinde, ed., *Non-verbal Communication*. Cambridge: Cambridge University Press

Curwen, C.A. 1972. 'Taiping Relations with Secret Societies and with Other Rebels', pp. 65–84 in Jean Chesneaux, ed., *Popular Movements and Secret Societies in China, 1840–1950*. Stanford: Stanford University Press

DeGlopper, Donald R. 1973. 'City on the Sands: Social Structure in a Nineteenth Century Chinese City'. Cornell University Ph.D. thesis
   1974. 'Religion and Ritual in Lukang', pp. 43–69 in Arthur Wolf, ed., *Religion and Ritual in Chinese Society*. Stanford: Stanford University Press

De Groot, J.J.M. 1885. 'Buddhist Masses for the Dead at Amoy', pp. 1–120 in *Actes du sixième congrès international des orientalistes tenu en 1883 à Leide, section 4, de L'Extrême-Orient*. Leiden: Brill
   1890. 'On Divination by Written Characters', *T'oung Pao*, 1: 239–47
   1969. *The Religious System of China: Its Ancient Forms, Evolution, History and Present Aspect*. 6 vols. Taipei: Ch'eng-wen. (Originally published 1892–1919)
   1970. *Sectarianism and Religious Persecution in China*. Taipei: Ch'eng-wen. (Originally published 1903)

Deliusin, Lev. 1972. 'The I-kuan Tao Society', pp. 225–33 in Jean Chesneaux, ed., *Popular Movements and Secret Societies in China, 1840–1950*. Stanford: Stanford University Press

Des Rotours, Robert. 1952. 'Les Insignes en deux parties (fou) sous la dynastie des T'ang (618–907)', *T'oung Pao*, 41: 1–148

Doolittle, Rev. Justus. 1872. *A Vocabulary and Handbook of the Chinese Language*. 2 vols. Foochow: Rozario, Marcal, and Company

Doolittle, Rev. Justus. 1966. *Social Life of the Chinese: with some account of their Religious, Governmental, Educational, and Business Customs and Opinions*. 2 vols. Taipei: Ch'eng-wen. (Originally published 1865)

Doré, Henry. 1965–7. *Researches into Chinese Superstitions*. Trans. M. Kennelly, D.J. Finn and Leo F. McGreal. 11 vols. Taipei: Ch'eng wen. (Originally published 1914–38)

Douglas, Carstairs. 1873. *Chinese–English Dictionary of the Vernacular or Spoken Language of Amoy*. London: Trübner and Company

Durkheim, Emile. 1915. *The Elementary Forms of the Religious Life*. London: George Allen and Unwin Ltd

Eberhard, Wolfram. 1970. 'Oracle and Theater in China', pp. 191–9 in *Studies in Chinese Folklore and Related Essays*. Indiana University Folklore Institute Monograph Series, vol. 23. Bloomington: Indiana University Research Center for the Language Sciences

Eitel, E.J. 1867. 'Spirit Rapping in China', *Notes and Queries on China and Japan*, 1: 164

Elliott, A.J.A. 1955. *Chinese Spirit Medium Cults in Singapore*. London: Royal Anthropological Institute

Fallers, Lloyd A. 1969. 'Bureaucracy in a Particularistic Setting', pp. 441–9 in Amitai Etzioni, ed., *A Sociological Reader on Complex Organizations*. New York: Holt, Rinehart and Winston

Feuchtwang, Stephan D.R. 1974a. *An Anthropological Analysis of Chinese Geomancy*. Vientiane: Vithagna

1974b. 'Domestic and Communal Worship in Taiwan', pp. 105–29 in Arthur P. Wolf, ed., *Religion and Ritual in Chinese Society*. Stanford: Stanford University Press

1974c. 'City Temples in Taipei under Three Regimes', pp. 263–301 in Mark Elvin and G. William Skinner, eds., *The Chinese City Between Two Worlds*. Stanford: Stanford University Press

1975. 'Investigating Religion', pp. 61–82 in Maurice Bloch, ed., *Marxist Analyses and Social Anthropology*. London: Malaby Press

1977. 'School-Temple and City God', pp. 581–608 in G. William Skinner, ed., *The City in Late Imperial China*. Stanford: Stanford University Press

Feuerwerker, Albert. 1975. *Rebellion in Nineteenth-Century China*. Michigan Papers in Chinese Studies No. 21. Ann Arbor: Center for Chinese Studies, University of Michigan

1976. *State and Society in Eighteenth-Century China: The Ch'ing Empire in its Glory*. Michigan Papers in Chinese Studies No. 27. Ann Arbor: Center for Chinese Studies, The University of Michigan

Finnegan, R. 1969. 'How to do things with Words: Performative Utterances among the Limba of Sierra Leone', *Man*, 4: 537–52

Fortes, Meyer. 1966. 'Religious Premisses and Logical Technique in Divinatory Ritual', *Philosophical Transactions of the Royal Society*. B, 251: 409–22

Freedman, Maurice. 1957. *Chinese Family and Marriage in Singapore*. Colonial Research Studies No. 20. London: Her Majesty's Stationery Office

Gallin, Bernard. 1966. *Hsin Hsing, Taiwan: A Chinese Village in Change*. Berkeley: University of California Press

Gamble, Sidney D. 1954. *Ting Hsien: A North China Rural Community*. Stanford: Stanford University Press

Geertz, Clifford. 1972. 'Deep Play: Notes on the Balinese Cock Fight', *Daedalus*, Winter: 1–37

Geisert, Bradley Kent. 1977. 'Superstition, the Kuomintang, and Local Elites in Kiangsu Province, 1927–1937', paper presented at the Sixth Annual Meeting of the Mid-Atlantic Region Association for Asian Studies

Giles, H.A. 1878. *A Short History of Koolangsu*. Pamphlet

1912. *A Chinese–English Dictionary*. 2 vols. Shanghai: Kelly and Walsh Ltd

Godelier, Maurice. 1977. *Perspectives in Marxist Anthropology*. Trans. Robert Brain. Cambridge: Cambridge University Press

Goody, E. 1972. ' "Greeting", "Begging", and the Presentation of Respect', pp. 39–71 in J. La Fontaine, ed., *The Interpretation of Ritual*. London: Tavistock

Goody, Jack. 1968. *Literacy in Traditional Societies*. Cambridge: Cambridge University Press

1976. *Production and Reproduction: A Comparative Study of the Domestic Domain*. Cambridge: Cambridge University Press

1977. 'Literacy, Criticism, and the Growth of Knowledge', pp. 226–43 in Joseph Ben-David and Terry Nichols Clark, eds., *Culture and its Creators: Essays in Honor of Edward Shils*. Chicago: Chicago University Press

Gray, John Henry. 1878. *China: A History of the Laws, Manners, and Customs of the People*. 2 vols. London: Macmillan

Grootaers, W.A. 1946. 'Une Société secrète moderne I-Koan-Tao bibliographie annotée', *Folklore Studies*, 5: 316–52

1951. 'Une Séance de spiritisme dans une religion secrète à Pékin en 1949', *Mélanges Chinois et Bouddhiques*, 9: 92–8

Bibliography

Hamberg, Theodore. 1935. *The Visions of Hung-Siu-tshuen, and Origin of the Kwang-si Insurrection.* Peiping: Yenching University Library. (Originally published 1854)

Harrell, Stevan. 1974. 'When a Ghost Becomes a God', pp. 193–206 in Arthur P. Wolf, ed., *Religion and Ritual in Chinese Society.* Stanford: Stanford University Press

  1979. 'The Concept of Soul in Chinese Folk Religion', *Journal of Asian Studies,* 38: 519–28

Hart, H.L.A. 1961. *The Concept of Law.* London: Oxford University Press

Hart, H.L.A. and A.M. Honoré. 1959. *Causation in the Law.* Oxford: Oxford University Press

Horton, Robin. 1960. 'A Definition of Religion, and its Uses', *Journal of the Royal Anthropological Institute,* 60: 201–26

  1967. 'African Traditional Thought and Western Science', parts I and II. *Africa,* 37: 50–71; 155–87

Hou Ching-Lang. 1975. *Monnaies d'offrande et la notion de trésorerie dans la religion chinoise.* Mémoires de L'Institut Des Hautes Etudes Chinoises, 1. Paris: Institut des Hautes Etudes Chinoises, Collège de France

Howe, James. 1977. 'Carrying the Village: Cuna Political Metaphors', pp. 132–63 in J. David Sapir and J. Christopher Crocker, eds., *The Social Use of Metaphor.* Philadelphia: University of Pennsylvania Press

Hsiao, Kung-chuan. 1960. *Rural China: Imperial Control in the Nineteenth Century.* Seattle: University of Washington Press

Huang Liu-hung. 1893. *Chü-kuan Fu-hui Ch'üan-shu* (Official Guide to Happy Rule). Chung-shu T'ang

Huc, M. 1970. *The Chinese Empire,* 2 vols. Port Washington, N.Y.: Kennikat Press. (Originally published 1855)

Hucker, Charles O. 1966. *The Censorial System of Ming China.* Stanford: Stanford University Press

Hunt, Ewa. 1977. 'Ceremonies of Confrontation and Submission: The Symbolic Dimension of Indian–Mexican Political Interaction', pp. 124–47 in Sally F. Moore and Barbara G. Myerhoff, eds., *Secular Ritual.* Amsterdam: Van Gorcum

Jarvie, I.C. 1964. *The Revolution in Anthropology.* London: Routledge and Kegan Paul

Jen Yu-wen. 1973. *The Taiping Revolutionary Movement.* New Haven: Yale University Press

Johnston, R.F. 1910. *Lion and Dragon in Northern China.* London: John Murray

Jordan, David. 1972. *Gods, Ghosts and Ancestors.* Berkeley: University of California Press

Keightley, David N. 1978. *Sources of Shang History: The Oracle-Bone Inscriptions of Bronze Age China.* Berkeley: University of California Press

Kiong, P. Simon. 1906. *Quelques mots sur la politesse chinoise.* Variétés Sinologiques No. 25. Shang-hai: Imprimerie de la Mission Catholique

Kleinman, Arthur. 1978. 'Comparisons of Patient–Practitioner Transactions in Taiwan: The Cultural Construction of Clinical Reality', pp. 329–74 in Arthur Kleinman, Peter Kunstadter, E. Russell Alexander and James L. Gale, eds., *Culture and Healing in Asian Societies: Anthropological, Psychiatric and Public Health Studies.* Cambridge, Mass.: Schenkman

Ku Tun-jou. 1966. 'Hsinchuang Village: A Study of a Taiwanese Village in the Political Context of Lunching Township', *Chinese Culture*, 7, 2: 65–106

Kuan-sheng-ti-chün Ying-yen T'ao-yüan Ming-sheng Ching (fu Sheng-ch'ien I-pai Shou) (The True Divine Scriptures Verified by the Lord Kuan-ti in the Peach Garden (with 100 Divine Lots)). 1971. Tainan, Taiwan: Fa-lun Shu-chu

Kuan-yin Ling-ch'ien (Kuan-yin's Efficacious Lots). N.d. Hong Kong: Wu-kuei T'ang Shu-chü

Kulp, D.H. 1925. *Country Life in South China*. New York: Teachers College, Columbia University

Lewis, D.K. 1969. *Convention*. Cambridge, Mass.: Harvard University Press

Lewis, I.M. 1971. *Ecstatic Religion: An Anthropological Study of Spirit Possession and Shamanism*. Harmondsworth: Penguin Books

Li Ch'un-feng. 1800. *Tseng-pu Wan-fa Kuei-tsung* (The Original 10,000 Methods, Revised and Enlarged). [Taoist Charms.] Fen-ya Tsang

Li Shih-yü. 1948. *Hsien-tsai Hua-pei Mi-mi Tsung-chiao* (Religions secrètes contemporaines dans le nord de la Chine). Studia Serica Monographs Series B: 4

Li Wei-tsu. 1948. 'On the Cult of the Four Sacred Animals (Szu ta men) in the Neighborhood of Peking', *Folklore Studies*, 7: 1–94

Lin Yueh-hwa. 1948. *The Golden Wing*. London: K. Paul Trench Trubner

Lindley, A.F. (Lin-le). 1866. *Ti-Ping Tien-Kwoh: The History of the Ti-ping Revolution, Including a Narrative of the Author's Personal Adventures*. London: Day and Son Ltd

Liu Chi-wan. 1974. 'Lü Lü-shan Chiao chih Shou-hun Fa' (Six Rites of the Lü-shan Sect for Recovering the Soul), pp. 207–372 in *Chung-kuo Min-chien Hsin-yang Lun-chi* (Essays on Chinese Folk Belief and Folk Cults). Taipei: Institute of Ethnology, Academia Sinica, monograph no. 22

Lu Chiu-ju. 1864. *Ying-ch'ou Hui-hsüan Hsin-chi* (On Etiquette with Model Letters). Chih-ya T'ang

McCreery, John. 1973. 'The Symbolism of Popular Taoist Magic'. Cornell University Ph.D. thesis

MacGowan, Rev. J. 1910. *Chinese Folk-lore Tales*. London: Macmillan and Company

MacInnis, Donald E. 1972. *Religious Policy and Practice in Communist China*. New York: Macmillan

Mao Tse-tung. 1965. *Selected Works*. vol. I. Peking: Foreign Languages Press

Marett, R.R. 1909. *The Threshold of Religion*. Third edn. London: Methuen and Company, Ltd

Marx, Karl and Frederick Engels. 1970. *The German Ideology*. C.J. Arthur, ed. New York: International Publishers

Mather, M.D. 1970. 'The Treatment of an Obsessive–Compulsive Patient by Discrimination Learning and Reinforcement of Decision-Making', *Behavior Research and Therapy*, 8, 3: 315–18

Medhurst, W.H., Compiler. 1853. *Pamphlets issued by the Chinese Insurgents at Nan-king; to which is added A History of the Kwang-se Rebellion, gathered from Public Documents; and a Sketch of the Connection between Foreign Missionaries and the Chinese Insurrection; concluding with A Critical Review of Several of the above Pamphlets*. Shanghai: N.C. Herald

Metzger, Thomas A. 1973. *The Internal Organization of the Ch'ing Bureaucracy:*

Legal, Normative, and Communication Aspects. Cambridge, Mass.: Harvard University Press

Moore, Omar Khayyam. 1957. 'Divination – A New Perspective', *American Anthropologist*, 54: 69–74

Morawetz, Thomas. 1973. 'Commentary: The Rules of Law and the Point of Law', *University of Pennsylvania Law Review*, 121: 859–73

Morgan, Harry T. 1942. *Chinese Symbols and Superstitions.* South Pasadena, Calif.: P.D. and Ione Perkins

Naquin, Susan. 1976. *Millenarian Rebellion in China: The Eight Trigrams Uprising of 1813.* New Haven: Yale University Press

Needham, Joseph. 1956. *Science and Civilization in China*, vol. II. *History of Scientific Thought.* Cambridge: Cambridge University Press

Novikov, Boris. 1972. 'The Anti-Manchu Propaganda of the Triads, *ca.* 1800–1860', pp. 49–63 in Jean Chesneaux, ed., *Popular Movements and Secret Societies in China, 1840–1950.* Stanford: Stanford University Press

Ortner, Sherry B. 1975. 'Gods' Bodies, Gods' Food', pp. 133–69 in Roy Willis, ed., *The Interpretation of Symbolism.* New York: John Wiley and Sons

Park, George K. 1963. 'Divination and its Social Contexts', *The Journal of the Royal Anthropological Institute*, 93, 2: 195–209

The Peking Gazette, Translation of 1873–1900. Shanghai: Reprinted from 'The North-China Herald and Supreme Court Consular Gazette'

Rappaport, Roy A. 1971. 'The Sacred in Human Evolution', *Annual Review of Ecology and Systematics*, 2: 23–44

　　1974. 'Obvious Aspects of Ritual', *Cambridge Anthropologist*, 2: 1.

Rawls, John. 1955. 'Two Concepts of Rules', *Philosophical Review*, 64: 3–32

Ray, Benjamin. 1973. 'Performative Utterances in African Rituals', *History of Religions*, 13, 1: 16–35

Ryle, Gilbert. 1958. 'A Puzzling Element in the Notion of Thinking', *Proceedings of the British Academy*, 64: 129–44

Saso, Michael R. 1972. *Taoism and the Rite of Cosmic Renewal.* Pullman, Wash.: Washington State University Press

　　1974. 'Orthodoxy and Heterodoxy in Taoist Ritual', pp. 325–36 in Arthur P. Wolf, ed., *Religion and Ritual in Chinese Society.* Stanford: Stanford University Press

　　1978. *The Teachings of Taoist Master Chuang.* New Haven: Yale University Press

Schipper. Kristopher M. 1974. 'The Written Memorial in Taoist Ceremonies', pp. 309–24 in Arthur P. Wolf, ed., *Religion and Ritual in Chinese Society.* Stanford: Stanford University Press

　　1977. 'Neighborhood Cult Associations in Traditional Tainan', pp. 651–76 in G. William Skinner, *The City in Late Imperial China.* Stanford: Stanford University Press

Schlegel, Gustave. 1866. *Thian Ti Hwui: The Hung-League or Heaven–Earth-League: A Secret Society with the Chinese in China and India.* Batavia: Lange and Company

Scott, James C. 1976. *The Moral Economy of the Peasant.* New Haven: Yale University Press

　　1977. 'Protest and Profanation: Agrarian Revolt and the Little Tradition, Parts I and II', *Theory and Society*, 4, 1 and 2: 1–38; 211–46

Seaman, Gary. 1974. 'Temple Organization in a Chinese Village'. Cornell University Ph.D. thesis

Bibliography

1981. 'The Sexual Politics of Karmic Retribution', in Emily Martin Ahern and Hill Gates, eds., *The Anthropology of Taiwanese Society*. Stanford: Stanford University Press

Searle, John. 1969. *Speech Acts: An Essay in the Philosophy of Language*. Cambridge: Cambridge University Press

1971. 'What is a Speech Act?', pp. 614–28 in Jay F. Rosenberg and Charles Travis, eds., *Readings in the Philosophy of Language*. Englewood Cliffs, N.J.: Prentice Hall

Shih, Vincent Y.C. 1967. *The Taiping Ideology: Its Sources, Interpretations, and Influences*. Seattle: University of Washington Press

Skinner, G. William. 1977. 'Cities and the Hierarchy of Local Systems', pp. 275–351 in *The City in Late Imperial China*. Stanford: Stanford University Press

Skorupski, John. 1976. *Symbol and Theory: A Philosophical Study of Theories of Religion in Social Anthropology*. Cambridge: Cambridge University Press

Smith, Arthur H. 1894. *Chinese Characteristics*. New York: Revell

1970. *Village Life in China*. Boston: Little, Brown and Company. (Originally published 1899)

Spence, Jonathan D. 1974. *Emperor of China: Self-portrait of K'ang-hsi*. New York: Knopf

Stanton, William. 1900. *The Triad Society or Heaven and Earth Association*. Hong Kong: Kelly and Walshe, Ltd

Tambiah, S.J. 1973. 'Form and Meaning of Magical Acts: A Point of View', pp. 199–299 in Robin Horton and Ruth Finnegan, eds., *Modes of Thought: Essays on Thinking in Western and Non-Western Societies*. London: Faber and Faber

Topley, Marjorie. 1953. 'Paper Charms and Prayer Sheets as Adjuncts to Chinese Worship', *Journal of the Malayan Branch of the Royal Asiatic Society*, 26, 1: 63–80

Van der Sprenkel, Sybille. 1962. *Legal Institutions in Manchu China*. L.S.E. Monographs on Social Anthropology, 24. London: Athlone Press

Vogt, Evon Z. 1952. 'Water Witching: An Interpretation of a Ritual Pattern in a Rural American Community', *Scientific Monthly*, 75: 175–86

Waismann, Friedrich. 1965a. 'Language Strata', pp. 226–47 in Anthony Flew, ed., *Logic and Language*. New York: Doubleday

1965b. 'Verifiability', pp. 122–51 in Anthony Flew, ed., *Logic and Language*. New York: Doubleday

Wakeman, Frederic. 1972. 'The Secret Societies of Kwangtung, 1800–1856', pp. 29–47 in Jean Chesneaux, ed., *Popular Movements and Secret Societies in China, 1840–1950*. Stanford: Stanford University Press

Wallace, Anthony F.C. 1966. *Religion: An Anthropological View*. New York: Random House

Walshe, W. Gilbert. N.d. *'Ways that are Dark': Some Chapters on Chinese Etiquette and Social Procedure*. Shanghai: Kelly and Walshe, Ltd

Ward, J.S.M. and W.G. Stirling, 1925. *The Hung Society or the Society of Heaven and Earth*, vol. I. London: The Baskerville Press, Ltd

Warner, John. N.d. *100 Years Ago: A Picture-Story of Hong Kong in 1870*. Hong Kong: The Government Printer

Watt, John R. 1972. *The District Magistrate in Late Imperial China*. New York: Columbia University Press

1977. 'The Yamen and Urban Administration', pp. 353–90 in G. William Skinner, ed., *The City in Late Imperial China*. Stanford: Stanford University Press

Weber, Max. 1947. *The Theory of Social and Economic Organization*. Trans. A.M. Henderson and Talcott Parsons. New York: The Free Press

Welch, Holmes. 1970. 'Facades of Religion in China', *Asian Survey*, 10: 614–26

Weller, Robert P. 1980. 'Unity and Diversity in Chinese Religious Ideology'. Johns Hopkins University Ph.D. thesis

Whyte, Martin King. 1974. *Small Groups and Political Rituals in China*. Berkeley: University of California Press

Wilhelm, Richard and Cary F. Baynes, trans. 1967. *The I Ching or Book of Changes*. Princeton: Princeton University Press

Williams, S. Wells. 1965. *The Middle Kingdom: A Survey of the Geography, Government, Literature, Social Life, Arts, and History of the Chinese Empire and Its Inhabitants*. 2 vols. Taipei: Ch'eng-wen. (Originally published 1883)

Wolf, Arthur P. 1974a. 'Gods, Ghosts and Ancestors', pp. 131–82 in *Religion and Ritual in Chinese Society*. Stanford: Stanford University Press

ed. 1974b. *Religion and Ritual in Chinese Society*. Stanford, Stanford University Press

Wu, Silas H.L. 1970. *Communication and Imperial Control in China: Evolution of the Palace Memorial System, 1693–1735*. Cambridge, Mass.: Harvard University Press

Yang, C.K. 1959. 'Chinese Bureaucratic Behavior', pp. 134–64 in D.S. Nivison and Arthur F. Wright, eds., *Confucianism in Action*. Stanford: Stanford University Press

1961. *Religion in Chinese Society*. Berkeley: University of California Press

Appendix: Character list

(H) = Hokkien   (M) = Mandarin

an-thai (H)	安	胎
Ang-kong (H)	翁	公
ang-pau (H)	紅	包
bou-hap (H)	沒	合
ce-bun (H)	祭	文
cha (M)	札	
Chen-chang (M)	鎮	長
ch'eng (M)	誠	
Ch'eng-huang (M)	城	隍
chiam (H)	籤	
ch'i (M)	氣	
chi-ping (M)	疾	病
chia (M)	甲	
chia-chai (M)	家	宅

chia : (H) 請

chiao (M) 醮

chiao-i (M) 交 易

chieng (H) 敬

Chieng-cui Co-su (H) 清 水 祖 師

chieng-sin (H) 正 神

chih-ling (M) 勅 令

chin kuan (M) 金 冠

ching (M) 敬

ch'ing shen (M) 請 神

chiong-tau (H) 冲 到

ch'iu-ts'ai (M) 求 財

ch'iu-yü (M) 求 雨

chou (M) 州

Chü-Shan-So (M) 聚 善 所

ch'u-ch'ien (M) 出 籤

ch'u-hsing (M) 出 行

chuan-ch'eng pai-yeh (M) 專 誠 拜 謁

ci-hu (H) 姐 夫

cieng (H) 正

Co-su-kong (H) 祖 師 公

e-e (H) 下 下

Character list

fa-shih (M)	法 師
fen-hsiang (M)	分 香
Feng-shui hsien-sheng (M)	風 水 先 生
fu (M) (charm)	符
fu (M) (prefecture)	府
gua-ke (H)	外 家
he-chiam (H)	火 籤
hi-guan (H)	許 願
hsiao pei (M)	笑 筊
hsieh-p'ien (M)	謝 片
hsien (M)	縣
hsin-jen (M)	尋 人
hsing-jen (M)	行 人
Hsiu-tsai (M)	秀 才
Hsueh Fu Ch'ien Sui (M)	薛 府 千 歲
hu (H)	符
huan (H)	犯
huan-guan (H)	還 願
hue (H)	會
hun-yin (M)	婚 姻
I Ching (M)	易 經
i-chu (M)	移 居

131

132

135

yin (M)

yu-yang (M)

yü (M)

yüeh-sung (M)

yun-t'u (M)

zip-tou (M)

陰 仰
右 訴
諭 途
越 道
運
入

Index

accessibility: direct appeals to higher officials and, 102–4; to gods, 81–2, 99–100, 101, 102; to officials, lack of, 81–2, 99–102
addressing, forms of, 33–7, 39
ancestors, 1, 29, 62; offerings to, 40; ultimate authority of, 86; worship of, 105–6
anxiety, divination and, 115–16
appeals: direct, to higher officials, 102–4; to gods, 2–4
Austin, J.L., 11
authority, 40, 106; ancestors and, 86; direct appeals to higher, 102–4; divination systems and, 86–91; of *gua-ke* at funerals, 13; interpersonal ritual and, 16; limits on (gods and officials), 95; local gods and, 84–5; obtained from gods, 36–7; possession and, 89–90; rank and spiritual, 93–4; sources of, for gods and officials, 94–5; of spirits, 29; spirit writing and, 90–1; true nature of, 92

bad days, avoidance of, 14
Baker, John Earl, 111 n. 1 (Chapter 2)
Bartlett, F.C., 116 n. 2 (Chapter 5)
Bascom, W.R., 86
Bateson, Gregory, 13
belief systems of peasants, 81
Bernstein, Basil, 114 n. 9
birds, lot choice and, 49
Black, Max, 97
Bloch, Maurice, 77, 78, 87, 88, 92, 106, 114 n. 9
blocks, *see* divining blocks (*pue*)

body positions, 39, 112 n. 2 (Chapter 3); change in closed ritual practice and, 73, 74; constitutive rule and, 67–8; *see also* gestures
Bohannan, P.J., 114 n. 12
Bourdillon, M.F.C., 78
bracketed communication, *see* communication, bracketed
bureaucracy: centralization and, 96; charms as communication to spiritual, 24–6, 27–8, 29; earthly and spiritual compared, 100–2; gift giving and, 38; peasant's knowledge of, 96; position of gods and ghosts in spiritual, 11, 29, 93, 95; similarity between spiritual and official, 16, 22, 23–4, 29, 36, 39, 92–6, 99–100; spiritual, 2, 23; Taoist priest's position in spiritual, 23, 36; of underworld, 118 n. 11; written communications of, 16–21

calling cards, proper use of, 21
canonization, 79–80, 82, 83
ce-bun (sacrificial essay), 21–2
character (written) analysis, 51
charms, 15, 16; avoidance of bad days and, 14; bureaucratic implications of, 24–6, 27; burning/eating of, 28; code of, 27–8; for curing illness, 36; magical effect of, 29–30; officials and, 26–7; as orders, 26–7, 28; paper, high gods and, 24; possession ritual and, 49–50; posting of, 28; as scare tactic, 28–9; secret sects and, 86; sets of, 26
Ch'en, Hsiang-ch'un, 28

Index

ch'i (breath), 15, 56
chiam, see thiu-chiam (asking for lots)
chiao ritual, 23–4, 29
Ch'ing dynasty, rituals of, on Taiwan, 106–7
Christian, William Armistead, 116 n. 1 (Chapter 6), 118 n. 9
Christianity, 74
Ch'ü, T'ung-tsu, 100
citizens: communications of officials with (written), 17–20; dichotomy between government officials and, 78; as gods, 80–1; power of state and, 98; relationship to officials and, 98–100; ritual and opposition to officials and, 92; see also peasants
closed practices: change in, 69–74; constitutive/regulative rules and, 67–9; defined, 64–6; divination procedures as, 65, 67, 91; divining blocks (pue) as, 67; games as, 65–6; learning and, 97, 98, 102, 104, 105–6, 110; official messages and, 88; pai-pai as, 67–8, 69–71; parliamentary process as, 65, 67; see also open practices
code(s), 110; charm, 27–8; chiam and, 60–2, 115; frozen shape of, 114 n. 10; geomancy and, 56–7; horo-scopic divination and, 57; I Ching and, 57; interpersonal divination and restricted, 53–6; interpersonal and non-interpersonal divination contrasts/similarities and, 53–4, 57–9, 62–3; non-interpersonal messages and, 56–7; prearranged, 68; regulative and constitutive rules of, 58–9; restricted, 53–6, 59–60
communication: bracketed, examples of, 12–13, 14; divination methods of communicating with gods and, 45–63; etiquette and, 31–7; as interpersonal transactions, the gods and, 4, 9–14, 16; non-interpersonal messages and, 56–7; as non-interpersonal transactions, the gods and, 9, 14–15, 53–6; restricted codes and, 53–6; written bureau-cratic, 16–20; written spiritual, 24–30; written unofficial, 20–1;

see also interpersonal communi-cation; non-interpersonal communi-cation
compass, geomancy and, 50, 53, 56
constitutive rules, see rules
control: etiquette and, 31–41; exchange of goods and, 37; of non-human beings, 4, 5; political, 16, 31, 109–10; social, 5, 87–8
Cormack, J.C., 24
corruption (official), underlings and, 100–2
Co-su-kong (god), 2, 63, 101
Croll, Elisabeth, 119 n. 17
crowds, fear of, by officials, 85
cults, see sects

deference, 35–7; see also politeness; respect
De Groot, J.J.M., 21, 24, 26, 117 n. 12
disputes: function of official docu-ments and, 19–20; officials and, 103
divination, 36; anxiety and, 115–16; authority and, 86–91; codes and non-interpersonal, 56–7; geomancy and, 50, 53, 56–7, 59, 63; hand-writing analysis and, 51; horo-scopic, 50–1, 53, 57, 63; inter-personal/non-interpersonal (con-trasted), 53–4, 57–9, 62–3; physiognomy and, 51, 53; possession and, 49–50, 54, 60; pue (divining blocks) and, 32, 45–7, 55, 59, 60; restricted codes and, 53–6, 59–60; thiu-chiam and, 47–9, 57, 59, 60–2; Tiv, 114 n. 12; tortoise shell and three coin, 49; traits of, 45
divination procedures: as closed prac-tice, 65, 67, 91; legitimacy and, 86; as open practice, 69; uniformity of, 95
divination slips, 55; topics on, 117 n. 5
divining blocks (pue), 32, 45–7, 55, 59, 60, 69, 70, 95; closed practices and, 67
Doolittle, Justus, 11–12, 27, 37, 38, 47–9, 50, 68, 71, 84
Doré, Henry, 57
dowry, 38
Durkheim, Emile, 16, 105

138

CAMBRIDGE STUDIES IN SOCIAL ANTHROPOLOGY

General Editor: Jack Goody

*Also published as a paperback